Embracing Your Mark of Authenticity

A Creed to Humanity

D1246313

Embracing Your Mark of Authenticity-

A Creed to Humanity

Copyright © 2013 by Jason E Renville

Library of Congress cataloging – in – publication Data

Published by Divine Intelligence Press

PO Box, 242363 Charlotte, NC 28224

Printed in the USA

Divine Intelligence Press

Presented to:

Date:

Nature of Occasion:

Acknowledgement

This project is underscored by a sequence of life events which have propelled me to this space that I now occupy. To be a student of life one must possess a teachable spirit. To learn from its many lessons one must incline his ear to wisdom and understanding. To everyone who has been a factor in the equation of my learning continuum, I am truly thankful for you.

This piece of literary work would have remained elusive, had it not been for the steadfast commitment of those who came along side me over the many years. Thank you for pouring into my life those virtues which I can never repay.

Thank you to my wife Jenny and children Judah, Victoria, and Jason. They are my biggest cheerleaders! To Reginald Yong a constant father figure in my life. To the Continuous Care Department at Vitas Innovate Hospice in Fort Lauderdale, Florida - your unwavering support and love you show every time a project is being born is second to none. To the Banquet Team of the Ballantine Hotel Charlotte, NC- you have come alongside me and offered unparalleled moral support and encouragement with this project. To my social media circle that has always shown an interest in my blogs, tweets and Facebook statuses – you encourage me even when I don't feel like writing.

To the task force which operationalized this project: PeriSean Hall, my multitalented editor. To Anthony Stilwell my graphic illustrator and web designer; to Aaron Quinn my video production / graphic designer- I could not have pulled this off without you on board.

Profound thanks, to all of the contributors to this work: Dwayne Nash, Ramando Horton, Deborah Collins-Threets, DelroySouden, Jeff Franz, Frankie Bobb–Semple, Martina Young and Robert Wesley Branch. The testament and total scope of this book would not have been as dynamic without the presence of your invaluable world views on authenticity.

To my friends, relatives and loved-ones whose presence in my life, which continues to inspire a standard of reaching for the highest expression of my authentic self, I am eternally grateful for you.

Dedication

To everyone who continually inspires a standard of reaching for the mark of authenticity, I salute you. To all those who are on a relentless quest of finding who they already are, do not stop until you identify, embrace and unleash the anatomy of your authenticity on every level of living. To you the reader, welcome to one of the greatest awakenings ever.

Embracing Your MARK of Authenticity
A Creed To Humanity

Author's Creed

Author's Creed

Make no apologies for your authenticity. Instead, you have to identify, embrace, develop, and unleash your authenticity relative to your life's assignment. The law of authenticity affords you the opportunity to manifest your genuine *GOD GIVEN* gifts, talents, passions, capabilities, ideas, and thoughts, (the way you were divinely created) without duplicating anyone and anything else. *YOU WERE CREATED TO BE AN ORIGINAL.*

CHAPTER 1

The Great Awakening

The Great Awakening

Authenticity is everything in anything; the essence of living an original life....It is the driving force of your distinct purpose, the exact thing that you were wired for in this lifetime, without trying to do or be like someone else.

There is *one* collective cry in the world today that echoes across Socio Cultural and Spiritual lines; it is the *CRY* for authenticity - life's original meaning! People everywhere want to know "who am I and what am I." Where do I fit in on the stage of life? Is there significance to my being here in this earth realm? How do I harness the power of my uniqueness to make that indelible mark on the world while serving humanity? All of these questions and more in relation to the original manifestation of our purpose occupy our thoughts every day.

I am of the persuasion that the presence of unhealthy duplication, confusion, misunderstandings, frustration, lack of creativity, lack of direction, misalignment of purpose, abuse of talents, gifts and abilities and every other "prison warden" that we allow in our lives which hold us captive and prevent us from living an authentic life, is directly the result of not discovering the true essence of life's original meaning – ***our authentic function here in this earth realm.*** This misunderstanding hinders the progressive and unique development of our trademark in life.

Authenticity is the art and science of being an original you – the genuine discovery and expression of who you really are! It means occupying the exact set place of your life's assignment that you were created to fulfill. In this global village in which we live: countries, cities, communities, organizations, corporations, churches, social clubs, homes, where ever individuals and wherever you can find a body, or groups of people, the posture of inauthenticity seems to be rising to a place of prominence in their lives. This is a direct reflection of the lack of understanding and application of the rules of living an original life. Why is this? Is it the lack of education, information, ingenuity, identity inspiration, or it is just the whole notion of a poor legacy of living from a mindset that was handed down to us?

The degree to which you understand and embrace your mark of authenticity relative to your life's journey here in the earth realm, it is to that same degree you will live a life that is full of inspiration, passion, meaning, flavor, zeal, creativity, wisdom, and vision. I call this level of consciousness, the realm where freedom begins. I say where freedom begins because many individuals are living in the grave of other people's suggestions, projections, judgments, options, thoughts, ideologies, ideas, and philosophies. It's as if they are waiting for permission from someone to live their lives, when in actuality their existence in the earth has been sanctioned by the Creator Himself.

Many such individuals never rise to the occasion of the "authentic expression of their true selves." And if you ask them about their original thoughts concerning their life, they really cannot give you an honest response. This type never takes the time to discover, embrace, develop, and celebrate their true hidden treasure; that is, the genuine essence and reputation of who they really are, exactly the way they were divinely created to express themselves.

When you find your place of authenticity, it is like holding a master-key which can unlock every door as you journey through life. Everything relative to your original purpose here in the earth realm will begin to flow synergistically.

I am writing this book to inspire a standard of authentic living, in hope of provoking people to reach deep down within themselves, and ask this question "Have I taken the full responsibility for managing my gifts, talents, and abilities, in such a way which will allow me to enjoy the holistic benefits of an authentic life?"

I call you to attention, to awaken every latent authentic stream which is already on the inside of you. It is my hope that you will no longer ask permission to live but you will embrace your mark of authenticity, as given to you by your Creator. It's time to unleash your authentic power from within.

Embracing Your Mark of Authenticity

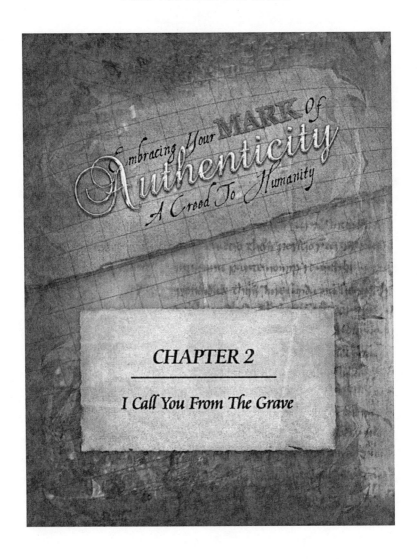

CHAPTER 2

I Call You From The Grave

I Call You From The Grave

I declare to you the reader, friends, and family – that you will posture yourself to really live authentically, and embrace your individuality IN THIS SEASON. I further speak, that you will begin to move in the direction of maximizing your entire God-given potential. My sincere prayer is that "you will progress past the place of conceptualization and experience your authentic destiny and purpose." I say to you that all the original juices that have been lying dormant on the inside of you will be actualized in this season of your life!

It has been said by *SO MANY* that one of the world's richest places still remains the graveyard - the place where some of the greatest thinkers, inventors, problems solvers, trendsetters, trailblazers, and world changers have been laid to rest. They never tapped and unleashed the fullness of their true potential. This is a sad reality to embrace, but it is the case. These individuals never tapped into their "treasure –chest" (their original God-given gifts, talents, and abilities) while they lived here in this earth. Life for them was just this: they were born, lived, died and were buried. The sequence of events and individuals which surrounded them were not congruent with their discovery and alignment to their place of authenticity.

The other striking phenomenon that plagues humanity more and more is that even though so many of us are not physically dead and buried, we suffer death in so many other forms and we are buried in several kinds of graves. Death to our dreams, visions, witty ideas, creative inventions, mission statements for life, desires, goals, and the very purpose for which we were created. We are buried in the graves of "what if", "I wanna be like so and so", "I wish I had a better life", or "I can't be like him or her." We wander around in "if only" and "wannabe land", and never rise to the occasion of embracing our true identity.

So many of us are walking around with a sense of lost identity. Somewhere along the course of life, some of us have been "high jacked and held hostage" by someone else's opinions or projections of us. In most instances we have arrested and locked ourselves in all kinds of prisons as well.

The reality is that we have to release ourselves from whatever state of imprisonment we find ourselves in. We possess the ***MASTER-KEY!*** As we transition our way out of prison we have to make sure we annihilate the "prison wardens" which held us up – ***take back your personal God-given power*** and superimpose the genuineness of your ***original God-given identity in your life.***

I believe that we originated from a Creator who is powerful, authentic, and limitless. We have been created in His image and likeness to produce after the same order. Whenever we find ourselves in a place of limitation, stagnation, or just caught up in the whirlwind of wanting to be someone else or wishing our lives away, we must remind ourselves that we are in total violation of our authentic nature – the genuine essence and reputation of who we were created to be in this earth. This astonishing and remarkable discovery has to be made by only you in order for you to be able to brand your true identity in the world today. You will have to realize that the keys of "authentic living" are right there in your hands. Just activate them...Use them for unlimited access to the infinite possibilities which are already on the inside of you. That is just how you are divinely created...embrace it! What an illuminating and transforming eternal journey to embark on...In this realm you are no longer asking for permission to live authentically. Rather, your consciousness is now being elevated, healed and restored to the degree of understanding that you are an authentic expression of your Creator in this earth realm. I believe it is at this breaking point, a place of awakening to the reality that everything you have ever dreamed or imagined for your life will begin to flow toward you with a clearer understanding of your life purpose. Every project, vision, mission statement, and dream that you endeavored to execute in your life, although seemingly difficult to launch, will come to fruition, if you only embrace your authentic anatomy (just by simply embracing your original design for your original purpose.) It takes a great deal of time and energy trying to be who you are not created to be, so why not use that same expanse of energy in the direction of building your life from a place of true meaning? So many of us become bitter, frustrated, and angry at ourselves and life, and we give up because we are not experiencing life like we want to.

I really believe this is a good place for you to evaluate and reassess the state of your progress in life from an authentic perspective. Forget the "cookie cutter" mind-set, the mold, the labels, and the box out of which you lived all your life. For once in your life allow your thoughts and ideas to flow from an uncontaminated and uninterrupted place from within. In order for you to manifest the genuine essence of who you are, you must detach from the external sources of validation that you think you need. Align your thoughts to your Creator's and allow the awakening of every authentic stream to rise and begin flowing from within.

Once this process of identifying and embracing your original self is set in motion – the Creator's Blue print for your life will begin to unfold right before your eyes. Now your energies and focus are in a whole new place. This will be a place, of discovery, creativity, ingenuity, discipline and cultivation of your life's assignment here in the earth realm.

Your endeavors, projects, vision, and dreams require time, energy and focus. When we step outside of our "authentic flow" and keep pouring energies and resources into areas that are counterproductive to the Creator's original intent for us, most times, we wind up tired, disoriented, irritated, and in some cases suffer all sorts of break-downs to our soul and physical bodies. Sometimes we are active but not productive; or as some people would say, "going through the motions." However, you are really not on that authentic course for your life; that path of meaning and purpose for which you have been created to travel.

The unfruitful cycle of being caught up in the whirlwinds of inauthenticity, can go on for a very long time, as your original self is poised and locked in an internal place of warfare crying out for its true expression. Silently there is a tug-of war between the ideal and the real, here you know you should be and where you actually are. What you are currently doing and what you want to do? What your inner gut feeling are relative to your purpose, versus the false labels of life which were embraced through the process of socialization and adaptation.

When you rise up and begin to let go of all baggage, weights, false-labels, projections, judgments, and erroneous paradigms that have stripped you of your true essence of living; you will begin to embrace your authentic self, produce your real purpose, your soul will be refreshed and renewed, and you will continually progress at the Creator's divine rate for your life. You will begin to experience the unimaginable relative to your true living essence, which takes you beyond every law of limitation regarding the mark of authentic on your life.

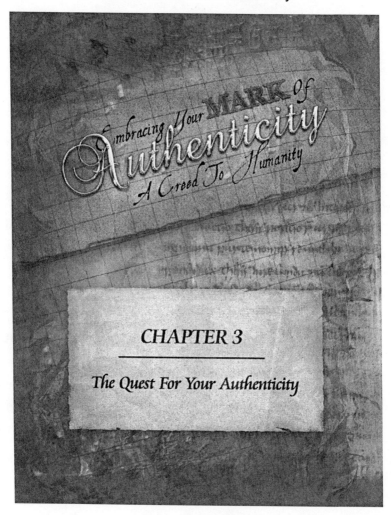

Embracing Your MARK of
Authenticity
A Creed To Humanity

CHAPTER 3

The Quest For Your Authenticity

The Quest for Your Authenticity

"The hardest battle you're ever going to fight is the battle to be just you." *Leo Buscaglia*[1]

The quest for authenticity is an age-old phenomenon. However much we might debate what the "quest for authenticity' is, it's all based on the many contributions and ideologies of notable philosophers and history makers. We have to conclude that the search for life's original meaning relative to our existence transcends every economic, social, racial class, and boundary. The quest for authenticity is probably the single most sought-after realm relative to the human existence. Everyone has interviewed themselves at some point by asking what I call the "three W's." Where did I come from? Who am I? And why am I here? Basically, we all want to find out the point of our lives, and

---

[1]Buscaglia, L. (n.d.). Wisdom quotes. Retrieved from http://www.wisdomquotes.com

how to discover and manifest the highest degree of our authentic selves.

It does not matter where you find yourself on the service gamut of life; this audible or silent quest for authenticity attends the souls of all in some way or other. From Kings and Presidents, to nations and neighborhoods, corporations, to the corner stores, noblemen, to civil service workers, families, or just a simple person, we all ask the same big question to ourselves about "self-significance" and embark on this intriguing or painful quest for authenticity. I believe that the crown of everything authentic, which we will discover and ever embrace about ourselves, lies within our legitimate pursuit to know who we really are and the measure of what we possess on the inside of us.

I am a firm believer that if you search hard and long enough for your mark of authenticity, you will find what you are looking for, and if you knock consistently and hard enough on the door of life, it will be opened for you. Many of us, from all walks of life, experience the different phases of life: holding patterns, shifting, discoveries, developments and awakenings. This cyclical process is what I refer to as the "quest continuum" relative to an authentic life. Let's take a quick journey through the different levels of questioning, embracing, and awakenings, to your authentic self to see where you can be located.

The Blank Stare:

I can distinctively remember when I first got an iPhone. I would hold it in my hands, click on one of the icons and just stare at it. I wasn't calling anyone, messaging, or on any form of social media - to tell you the truth, I couldn't really give you a concrete reason as to why I was doing this, I was just aware that I was. I was just looking at a device with a blank stare. I repeated this pattern time after time until it became a cycle. It was almost as if I had fallen into a catatonic state doing this. Sound familiar?

This is exactly the sequence of events that play out in many of our lives on a daily basis while we are on the quest for authenticity. We know for sure that we have been given the gift of life because we get up every day and can sense that there is more to life than just waking up to a mundane routine and then going back to bed at night. The feeling of not managing our space well enough resonates deep within our souls and oftentimes plagues us silently as we go about our daily activities. Lastly, as we do this thing called life with a blank stare we then ask ourselves silently, "What is it I really want to do with my life that would make it count for something?"

In The Shadows of Others:

I was preparing for my first ever television appearance and I was kind of nervous. I am thinking to myself, what am I going to say, what am I going to wear, who do I want to sound like, after all people need a point of reference because no one knows me. So I called a friend of mine who has extensive experience in broadcast media to seek advice. The first thing she said to me was *"be yourself"*, she said "You don't have to sound and dress like anyone else to make an impression, people can sense originality and that is what they are looking for." When I finally got to the set on the day of the broadcast – just before we went live on air, the interviewer told me almost the same thing: "relax and be yourself."

Too many of us have a hard time being ourselves because we don't even know ourselves. We do not encourage or nourish ourselves long enough to really find out who we really are. We have no personal flavor or distinction for life. This in turn can disqualify us from that place of having an authentic identity. We find ourselves in a place of living in the shadows of other people's lives: we dress, speak, walk, and look like others; and if it were possible, some of us would even want to think like other people. Who has really figured out this thing about living authentically?

This insatiable desire to "live in the shadows of others" or wanting someone else's personal identity or lifestyle. This neutralizes our ability to embrace our "original trademark for our own lives." This desire stems from feelings of inadequacy and oftentimes reduces us to the lowest denominator on the "quest continuum" to the point where we need to replicate everything someone else does – we just want to do it like them. Many who are trapped in that realm sincerely believe that duplicating someone else's true pattern for living is the highest and best form of expressing themselves authentically, as they know it to be in that moment.

The Voice(s):

There are so many voices at play every day in our lives – the voice from within and the voices from without. The two combined can be quite a force to be reckoned with when the authentic self is caught "smack dead" in the middle. Which voice sways you? After all, most of the voices from within have been given to you through your upbringing, so how could you not choose that familiar path which has been chosen before by many and they turned out ok? On the other hand the projections and suggestions which flood the gates of our souls from our external environment are too numerous to mention. Everyone claims to have the voice which will steer you to the path of authentic living, "do this or do that." In the scheme of things, these are the questions I really want to ask you. Where is your voice? Have you ever stopped to tune into the frequency of your own voice?

As you discover the power of your own voice, it will speak loudly and clearly on your behalf. When you express your true self, you will be automatically yoked with your authentic course in life and every voice that contradicts your true self will eventually be silenced and rendered powerless. Your original voice will communicate and serve as the bridge between you and the greater purpose and vision you have been called to serve.

The Great Cover Up:

We are masters of getting under the covers; this is almost a natural response for so many of us. We cover up ourselves with so much of what is not our true nature, this, the search for who we are authentically becomes even more painstaking and illusive. Every so often, in an effort to express ourselves authentically, we end up reaching for the crutches which give us every reason to not live authentically.

One of the major cover-ups society has trained us to utilize is to always project an ideal image and keep the real one on the back burner; this way we protect ourselves from the judgments and rejection of others. In this case, there is no room for vulnerability and transiency for our authentic person. Many on the outside looking in want the "ideal life" that is projected, particularly if it's an image coming from mainstream media: a movie star, model, a talk show host, singers, or other personalities appearing in reality TV shows. Sometimes people aspire to become many of these things outside their authentic selves. This type of cover-up sometimes breeds all sorts of infections and dysfunctions. – Some will even lust for fame, power, prestige, and money, even at the expense of destroying others.

The next big thing for many of us, when living in the comfort zone of the great cover-up, it's always previewed as the safest way to go for some people. It shelters them from really taking true responsibility for living life authentically, because after all it really doesn't require any extra push. When you become complacent you lose the desire to break out beyond that realm; even though everything on the inside of you, which is there for you to express yourself authentically, is crying out for expression.

<u>Going Around In Circles:</u>

A "biggie" for so many of us is jumping from the in-crowd to the out-crowd, rubbing shoulders, and always looking for the next social event to provide us with a temporary "fix or high." This is all in an effort to either escape from the journey of locating "the real you", or to gain the favor or approval from someone or something outside of ourselves. I do not believe that there is anything wrong with being a part of something that's larger than you. I believe this is the essence of true service. However, at the same token, whenever you attempt to satisfy your thrust for an authentic life with external avenues, you initiate cycles of codependence, disappointment and disillusionment. This behavior can cause you to enter a realm of a lifelong search for meaning and significance; as a result, you could end up never arriving at your intended destination.

Whenever you bring to any relational circle the "whole you – the authentic you" it creates a balance for the intended purpose of that relationship. You are no longer going around in circles as a fragmented individual, with all of the underlying issues; you bring to the table of life. The very issues which do not contribute in a wholesome way to relationships developed along the path to discovering your life's meaning. Conversely, when you bring to the table your gifts, talents, and abilities in the spirit of service this increases the value of everything and everyone around you.

You've Been Approved:

Whose stamp of approval or validation are you waiting for before you can rise to the occasion of embracing all that you already are? Is it the right spouse, friend, club, group, church or organization?

Many of us are guilty as charged with this crime: we continue to cultivate relationships that are inauthentic and toxic in nature. We stay around people and places, who do not celebrate, encourage, enhance, develop, or increase the mark of authenticity on our lives. Healthy relationships, which will help us to grow and support our own identity, find their roots in the *law of reciprocity and mutuality* **(boundaries which are equally beneficial for all parties involved),** You should never be drained, depleted, or diluted on any level in any relational circle while fulfilling your original life assignment.

Major Violations:

Many times we find ourselves very angry and disappointed in other people because they have done something to us which hurt our feelings, or violated us in some way or other. In some instances, you might have legitimate reasons for your feelings. However, I want to take you on a different path of reasoning for a quick second. Most of what we cry about on a daily basis and refer to as people violating us is the result of having ***no healthy boundaries for our own lives.*** We violate ourselves in a major way by not ***discovering ourselves,*** and as a result, we are not able to declare and demonstrate to people who we really are. Whenever you invest the time to discover and establish that you are an authentic living being, you will be a beacon of light to those around you. As you live your authentic life, you will be able to define clear parameters for the operating system of your original place of assignment in life.

As you discover who you are, you will automatically create a different value system for your life. Your true perception of yourself, no doubt, will be elevated to the place where it should have been all along. You will find yourself establishing healthy boundaries in order to preserve and sustain this new discovery of your authentic worth. This is the quality and expanse of energy you will bring to anything you become a part of, which will leave little room for external violators and offenders.

The Wilderness:

The "wilderness" experience translates into so many things for so many people while on the quest for authenticity. The wilderness can refer to a place of breaking, discovery, embracing, contemplation, character building, conscious awakening, and even a place where destinies are aligned. I believe we discover things about ourselves in the "wilderness of life", without which we would not have discovered our life course.

There is no other life practicum that is as crucial as the wilderness experience. Why is this so? Oftentimes, this journey through the wilderness has to be made alone in order for you to derive the full benefits of the total experience. Although, you might be involved with your day-to-day activities, the wilderness experience is designed for only you to identify and embrace your mark of authenticity in life. You might not know it to be the wilderness as I am describing it here. But you know it more than anyone else; that place of aloneness which forces an incubator for discovering your true life's purpose.

Think of the times when you said to yourself "enough is enough, there is more to life than just this" and "I am going to really find out why I am placed here on this earth." Subsequently, you took off on a journey with every intention of finding meaning for your life. This is where you come face-to-face with yourself as no one else is occupying this space with you. You are locked in "the wilderness" by yourself until you decide to respond to the authentic call on your life. If you do not respond, the cycle repeats itself throughout the course of your life.

<u>The Big Invitation:</u>

The realm of authenticity has extended an open, eternal invitation to all humanity. Responding to the invitation of authenticity will center everything in your life. However, you have to personally respond in order to make sure that your individual identity does not lose its significance and meaning while you are yet alive. I believe with all of my heart, that the simplest to the most sophisticated of individual gets the invitation to live life authentically. At no point in life, could you say the opportunity was never presented. Many times we are not aware that it is an invitation because of the clutter of life.

Whether you realize it or not, everything in and around you is working to lead you to that place. We are invited to our authentic place throughout our life lessons: every test and tribulation, trial and triumph, disappointment, and victory, and highs and lows are all a part of the invitation. Your past, present, and future were already taken into consideration when the invitation was extended. This is how impartial this realm operates.

The Great Awakening:

Have you ever been doing something for a long time then you finally woke up one day and really became conscious of the fact that you were harming and not helping yourself? Once you answered that question, did you wonder "What in the world was I thinking?" It's like a light came on somewhere in your psyche. At this point you can begin to take steps to regain your ground.

Embracing the mark of your authenticity is one of the greatest awakenings the human soul will ever experience. This is the place where you establish your independence from the layers and labels of life which have prevented you from being yourself. Simply by living long enough, and buying into beliefs which are incongruent to who you are, and the extent to what you can accomplish can lock you out of the realm of authenticity - all by your own choosing!

These facets of formation can sometimes reduce you to a fraction beneath your real potential or even outright lie to you, telling you that you could not elevate to an authentic lifestyle. In some instances these images have been projected on your mind so much that you have to literally make a conscious effort to utilize the law of ***displacement and replacement***, (superimposing truth, wisdom, and knowledge over those mind-sets, which were previously cultivated that did not enable the expression of your authenticity to come forth in its purest of form) in your everyday life.

<u>Branding your Name:</u>

I was asked on several occasions on interviews, "Who do you want people to know you as" or "What do you want to be known for." I remember sitting there thinking "Do they really have to ask that?" As I became more mature as the years went by, I started realizing the power of branding your name. Whenever you rise up and announce to the public that you are authentic, people generally want to know "***who are you?***"

Your name is far more than what you're called or how you are identified. The true embodiment of your name is your essence, reputation and presence; the weight of how you are known or will be known as. Branding your name correctly is the lifeline of your authentic life. One of the questions most people should ask themselves on the quest for authenticity is, "How do I want to be known in this life time?" It has been said that a "good name is better than silver and gold." Another familiar saying is "your name will precede you."

Let's take for instance if you were to mention the following names in public: Michael Jackson, who is known as the King of Pop; Dr. Maya Angelo, a notable educator and poet; a living legend of wisdom, Bill Gates – the guy that developed and introduced Microsoft Windows to the World; LeBron James or Michael Jordon – two of the greatest basketball players of all times, whose names invoke the essence, presence, and memory of what they are known for, even if they are dead or alive.

You are no different as an individual; it doesn't matter where you find yourself on the spectrum of service in life. You don't have to be one of the superstars or someone in the limelight in order to brand your name authentically. You have been uniquely wired to brand your *OWN* name, the true core and spirit of who you were created to be. In order to brand your name with its true mark of distinction, it is your responsibility to find out all of the resources you already possess and how you want to utilize them in concert with your authentic life's assignment.

As You Reflect

After reading through this chapter, the obvious is occurring right now. You have either located yourself on one of the levels of what I call the quest "quest continuum" for your original purpose, or you are saying to yourself "Where do I begin with all of this." Do not allow yourself to become overwhelmed or disillusioned about processing all of this information at once. The most important factor right now for you is that you have identified where you are in the process, which is the beginning of the rest of this ecstatic journey of embracing your anatomy of authenticity. I guarantee that by the time you reach the end of this book you will be plugged into the realm of authenticity for yourself.

Embracing Your Mark of Authenticity

I have not forgotten those of you who might have already embraced your mark of authenticity. This chapter primarily served as a tool of reflection, introspection, inspiration and a reminder about what it takes to arrive at that place. My admonition to you is to always be an ambassador of authenticity. Whenever you are deployed into the different spheres of life by this realm, allow your original essence to permeate any atmosphere you find yourself in. This will provoke and inspire others who are on the "quest for authenticity" to make that *SHIFT* that would lead them to where you are - *in the realm of authenticity.*

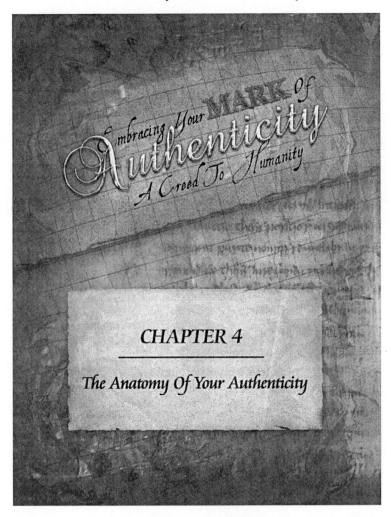

CHAPTER 4

The Anatomy Of Your Authenticity

The Anatomy of Your Authenticity

"But when you personalize your life, when you make your life a place where you can be yourself, when you do things the way you want to do them, your life feels like your home. And that is a tremendous source of emotional energy."

Mira Kirshenbaum [2]

The mode of operation for living an authentic life is very simple; there's nothing whimsical or mystical about it – you just have to make a conscious decision that you will embrace it at all costs. I call it the mark of authenticity you were born with, an inherent divine mark stamped on your life by your Creator. Everyone living on the face of the earth is wired and destined for an original purpose that only they can rise to the occasion to fulfill. The journey begins

---

[2]Kirshenbaum, M. (n.d.). Wisdom quotes. Retrieved from http://www.wisdomquotes.com

when you decide that you are no longer going to allow another force to dictate to you what you believe in your heart is your life's assignment, as mandated by your Creator.

I remember watching the Larry King Live TV Show when he interviewed Oprah Winfrey, shortly after she endorsed Barack Obama for President of the United States of America. One of the questions Larry King asked her was "Would you run for office?" Paraphrasing her response to him, she said *"No because the platform that I hold to speak to the world is of far more value to me."* In essence, she said that the world was her authentic place of assignment and she wasn't going to trade that for anything.

Oprah's remarks during an interview at the 2010 Kennedy Center Honors Award Show echoed the same sentiments she expressed on the Larry King Show: *"Be yourself, all of life is about becoming more of who you are, and you can be a better you than you can be anybody else. I started out pretending to be Barbara Walters and later figured out that I could be a better Oprah. So my best advice is to always to find a way to your true-self - to the highest truest expression of your true-self because that's what people are looking for, is your own individuality and uniqueness. That really has been it, if I were to say a secret to my success, that's been it."[3]*

Dr. Myles Monroe - one of the world's leading authorities on Human Development, even highlighted this simple, yet profound, subject matter of "individual authenticity" In His book Principles and Power of Vision. *"Do not ever allow anyone to cause you to think of yourself as ordinary. If anyone makes you feel less than you are, just look you self in the mirror and say. "You original thing you" You are one of a kind, irreplaceable, original. There is no one like you on earth. God made you that way because He wanted you to be perpetually rare."[4]*

---

[3] Winfrey, O. (2010). Oprah Winfrey for President, Retrieved from http://www.youtube.com/watch

[4] Monroe, M. (2003).The Principles and Power of Vision. New Kensington, VA.: Whitaker House

William Shakespeare, the great English poet is quoted as saying "*To thy own self be true.*"[5]

So many other individuals from continent to continent throughout the ages have arisen to the occasion of challenging humanity to live life that is inspired by the principles and patterns of authenticity. Yet this is probably one of the worst epidemics of the human race today, people living inauthentic lives.

It is obvious from the forgoing world views on authenticity by several of the world's influential people and shapers of authentic living that the principles and power of authenticity are not just abstract, but they are also practical in nature. This can be incorporated in our daily lives, if we only allow our consciousness to be awakened to its fullest. I believe that your anatomy of authenticity is crying out even now for expression in the purest of its form in your life. I also believe that you are searching for that vein in your life from which to operate. This is the road where

---

[5]Shakespeare, W. (n.d.). Shakespeare quotes. Retrieved from www.enotes.com

original purpose and relentless pursuit will merge to create a fusion - the path to life's original meaning.

Whether you know it or not trapped on the inside of you is an authentic person waiting to emerge, you were born to do something in this life time no one else has ever done. Also the way you were wired to do that assignment is unique. The proof of your uniqueness - this priceless treasure is encrypted in your *DNA*. From a scientific perspective your DNA contains vital and distinctive information about your inherent characteristics and traits.

This same inherent principle holds true about the *DNA* of your individual purpose. At birth you received the capacity and enablement to reproduce authentically on the outside what was already downloaded on the inside of you by your Creator. This download included all of your unique gifts, talents, visions, dreams, passions, and desires.

You can search from now until all eternity you will never find another you. The hair on your head, your facial features, your arms, your legs, the color of your skin, your finger prints, and everything else about your physiology, were made to perfection by your Creator. No one else, among the approximately seven billion people on the face of the earth, can be found with the exact same features and traits. This is a high point for celebration; I mean what a mark of distinction that is on every individual's life yet this mark is rarely discovered, cultivated and celebrated. For so many living an authentic life seems so far-fetched and unattainable.

What ends up happening in some cases, is that they foster relationships and stay in situations and circumstances which do not promote growth in their "original skin"- the "real them". A friend of mine,PeriSean Hall –the "Word Doctor" is quoted as saying ***"Being uncompromisingly real with yourself and others attracts right people and even if wrong people show up, they can't stay long! Don't ever place your authentic self on the shelf".*** I believe this is a powerful statement and expression of truth which needs to get in the hearts of all humanity. Too many people continue to cultivate relationships and paradigms that are not authentic in nature. They stay around people and situations that do not celebrate, encourage, enhance, develop, or increase their authentic essence. Sometimes they do not ever come out from that place – and as sad as it is, they die right there. I am not necessarily referring to physical death in this context. I am referring to that place where you are cut off from original meaning – where purpose and passion for your life is far removed from you, as far as the east is removed from the west.

On the other hand some people believe that the realm of authenticity is only reserved for specific groups of people – maybe the wealthy, the influential, the educated, or the privileged. This notion couldn't be further from the truth. The truth of the matter is that you can be all of these things, which sometimes can be used as a crutch to life or some of validation and yet not tap into the authentic you. So is living authentically relegated to a specific group of people? Absolutely not!

Authenticity is an equal opportunity employer. It is a Universal principle and pattern created and established by our Creator, which affords us the opportunity to manifest the genuineness of who we really are created to be. Individuals must fully assume responsibility for the lives they have been given to live here in this earth realm, even though life assignments in the earth realm have been authenticated by the Creator of all things. You, as an individual still have to remain actively involved with employing the rules of engagement relative to your personal authentic destiny.

What is the anatomy of your original trademark in life? Have you ever stopped long enough to asked yourself? The Creator has intelligently created the Universe and placed you in it – this is the highest and most significant investment that can be found. That's you! That is why you should be in a state of ever celebrating who you are as an individual. What makes you the crown of your Creator's Universal design? It is simply your specific difference that you bring to the table. You must know and embrace this simple truth: you were created the sole visionary and custodian of the degree of authenticity that you manifest in this lifetime.

If you are ever going to make your life count for something, you must rise up and accept the challenge of realizing your authenticity at all costs. No one is specifically wired for your life's purpose and you are not wired for anyone else's assignment. This challenge speaks loudly every day to everyone everywhere. It transcends color, creed, race, gender, age, and economic status. Everyone has a part to play in the grand scheme of things in this "big ole world."

Think about this simple yet profound phenomenon- If everyone was a Lawyer, Doctor, Scientist, School Teacher, Engineer, Law Enforcement Officer or Fashion Designer, then who would teach our children in school? Who would put out the many fires on a daily basis? Who would examine and diagnose what's wrong with you when you are ill? Who would serve all of the other varying needs of society at large? Then it is safe to conclude that authenticity is the driving force of accomplishing individual assignments, and is a contributing factor to the grand scheme of things in society. Even though authentic living fosters your individual "trademark" we are still inter–dependent. When authenticity is fully embraced and unleashed in its proper context, you will never have to worry about losing yourself in anything or for anyone. Authenticity will accentuate and preserve your unique gifts, talents, abilities, vision and dreams for your life.

The Anatomy Of Your Authenticity

In my own life I heard the cry of authenticity from within the very fibers of my being and did not know what it was. During that time I took a lot of internal trips, had a lot of day dreams, my imagination was stretched far and wide, had visions and saw pictures of so many things I could not really explain.

Ever since I was a child I felt a sense of purpose beyond just living from day-to day. I always felt as though I was born to do something, but it was hard to explain this to anyone. That "something" would tug at me from time to time. Of course, at that time I had no one that I could talk to about what I was feeling on the inside.

There was a vast dichotomy between my world within and my world without. My external environment growing up as a child did not, or could not support my belief system relative to my authentic course in life. I would constantly be on the lookout for that voice, that person or that moment to provide some source of affirmation and/or validation to the many dreams and visions which I pondered in my heart. The silent quest for meaning and significance became even more pronounced as I grew older. I embarked on a lifelong search...I had so many voices speaking to me and so many sources influencing me. At the end of most of my days I asked myself this one question, "Where do I really belong." I endured this agony well into my adolescent years and my early twenties.

I remember being at school not being sure of what would become of my career. I was very good at the Social Sciences and Home Economics. Home Economics was a natural for me because I was raised in an environment where household chores were inevitable. I quickly gravitated to the kitchen where I spent a considerable amount of time doing my household chores. When I finished high school, I attended a Culinary School after which I graduated and landed a job as a cook in my country (Guyana) at the Pegasus, the number one International Hotel. To many I appeared to have enjoyed it – and I did to a degree, but I knew it was not the total scope of my life assignment. There was still a void on the inside of me. A new episode of my internal unrest began all over again.

I decided to attend the University of Guyana where I was pursuing studies in Tourism and Hospitality. I thought that since I am in the hotel industry already, why not? While attending the University I worked overnight with the hope that one day I would be promoted to management. I quickly released the notion of that kind of promotion because it was just a figment of my imagination and it was not going to happen in the near future. I began to expand my mind and explore my options beyond where currently was. I still was searching to find who I was – my own VOICE.

In 2001, I entered a student exchange program in Hospitality which afforded me the opportunity of coming to the United States. By this time I thought to myself 'Wow – the land of opportunity, everything will be ok now.' I completed the first segment of the program in Jackson Hole, Wyoming which was an awesome experience. The second and final segment was done in Chicago, Illinois, which I enjoyed very much but it still it wasn't my destination. I knew it was just another bridge in life.

One of the things I had going for me, which I enjoyed very much was wherever I worked I had *"influence"* with people across the board, from the owners of the businesses, executive mangers, line -workers or just simply the co-workers in my department. I held a place of influence in people's lives. This simply just came from   being me. People would literally come to me with their personal life issues and business matters and just pour out their heart to me – it did not matter if I knew them for a day or a year. For some reason they felt comfortable.

People always had my undivided attention. I would offer comfort, counsel, wisdom, encouragement, my opinion and even help some of them to explore options for the situations and circumstances they were facing. They would always respond "Wow, which is exactly what I needed to hear, I see why I had to come to you." To me, it was just simply service: lending a listening ear or offering a word of encouragement.

I always wondered why in the world people would pass up going to the Human Resource Department, their own friends, or even their loved-ones to come to me. However, the feeling I got from encouraging, inspiring and empowering another human being was absolutely indispensable and beyond explanation. That feeling was the one constant, which always ignited my passion for living and reason for being. I still did not always like what I did as a Cook, Server, Front Desk Agent, Night Auditor, and Hospice Staffing Coordinator, but nonetheless, whatever position I held I displayed the best work ethic possible. At one point in my life, I had even resigned myself to the possibility that my life assignment was to work in these different positions to encourage, inspire, to bring life and hope to other people. I knew even then, I was not plugged into one hundred percent of my purpose.

I was an excellent researcher and reader, but I took it to another level when I realized that people from different walks of life would come to talk to me. I wanted to understand different cultures, philosophies, ideologies and paradigms which influenced the way people behave so that I could be more effective when relating to different people. In the course of my quest for meaning I saw myself authoring books, although early on I thought becoming an author was farfetched. As I mentioned to you earlier I enjoyed inspiring, motivating, encouraging and empowering people. After a while, writing came naturally but it was definitely not a part of my equation.

In 2006, while living in Miami, Florida, I started suffering from a very dark depression, to say the least. I have gone through several life changes, crises and transition in this lifetime, but this dimension of darkness was beyond my human comprehension and anything else that has ever attended my soul. I felt as though I was in a catatonic state, hopeless, and void of any real reason for living at the time.

On the outside I appeared to be fine to people, but on the inside it was pure misery –I was either one step away from walking in front of a car or taking some pills to end my life. The odd thing was that even though I was in that dark place –the silent quest for meaning and authenticity always remained. At one point, as dark as I felt, the voice of authenticity and meaning for life cried just as loud from within me. This definitely intensified the conflict from within. After all, this equation does not add up. At one level it felt as though my world within and without was coming to an end. On the other hand, I felt as though I was giving birth to a dimension of something that did not have a name or face. I just felt I was being stretched on every level. This cycle continued until about 2008.

I suffered from insomnia for a while and I remember clearly the degree of restlessness from one night in particular. It was very intense. It was about 2am that morning when I got up and started pacing the floors. It was as though I had come to the end of myself, literally. I remembered crying out and praying with a loud voice for God to lift my soul from whatever it was that caused that degree of darkness. About a half hour after, I literally felt a force guiding me to my computer room. As I was sitting on my chair, I felt this darkness lifting from me. I felt a shift almost immediately in my spirit and soul. It was at that place where I gave birth to my first book, "Bring My Soul Out of Prison."

As I sat in that chair, I started writing immediately and the flow was unbelievable. For the first time in my life I felt truly authentic and empowered. I felt as though I was elevated to a place where I was given utterance to authorship. I felt as though I had been granted access into the archives of Heaven, to say the least. I embraced it and knew that it was not up for negotiation or trade. The expanse of energy and revelation surrounding that moment was definitely unquantifiable. I felt as though I had given birth to a brand new dimension of life, meaning, significance, and purpose. By no means am I advocating that I was instantaneously catapulted to the fullness of my purpose; rather, I began to experience all there was to experience at that moment. I had enough discernment to know that I was plugged into a place that I have never been plugged into before in my entire life.

I don't believe that authoring books is all there is to my life's assignment, but it was through writing my first book that I began to have a working understanding of who I was really created to be. I believe that my general life's work is through writing, speaking, teaching and empowering individuals to identify, embrace, develop and unleash their authentic life; thus, maximizing their potential. There may be many other forms of expression that I will probably utilize as I continue to grow into and own my authentic space in this life.

It is an absolutely empowering experience to behold and to become your authentic self on the progression continuum…I believe once your authentic anatomy is activated, discovering and emerging into your authentic self-will becomes a lifelong phenomenon. As you grow through life processes and consciously respond to life lessons, those experiences will become the perfect recipe for sustaining your authentic essence and nature. Then the opportunities for discovering the many dimensions which will foster and establish you as a unique individual expression of life will become limitless.

These are some master-keys and foundational pillars to discovering, developing, and sustaining *YOUR AUTHENTIC WORTH!*

- Your true *identity* is the foundation for everything at this juncture of your life. You must identify your place of authenticity relative to your life's purpose. Equally as important are those specific resources that are around and available to you that will foster the birthing of an "authentic you."

- You must *embrace* your mark of authenticity without fear, if you are going to manifest the highest expression of who you really are. Whatever you embrace is given permission to embrace you.

- You must *invest* in the development of your authentic self in order to sustain longevity relative to your original life's assignment. You have to invest time, patience with yourself and others, strategic resources, and money.

- You have to be willing to *excavate* – dig deep, give yourself no rest if you have to, in order to discover your authentic treasures, which are already on the inside of you. Look no further!

- You have to be able to exercise some degree of *leadership* in the process of embracing your authentic assignment; it takes the leader in you to effectively translate and enforce authenticity to the different facets of your life's purpose.

- You must be able to discern and encourage your authentic *desires* relative to the blue print for your life.

- You must understand that *time* will provide several opportunities – windows, doors, and openings for you to make an authentic statement in life.

- You must be able to employ wisdom at all times to *execute* strategies and tactics which will lead to your authentic desired outcomes in life.

- You have to *motivate* and accentuate the authentic streams in your life. Motivation will serve as the driving force and center for everything authentic in your life.

- You have to bring some degree of *vulnerability* to the table of authenticity. Your willingness to be vulnerable opens you up to experience the many changes, channels, and outcomes which are all a part of the equation for living an original life.

- Your intensity and quality of *passion* for life will unleash authenticity on every level. Once authentic passion is given way in your life, you will ask yourself questions like- Who am I? Why am I here? What am I really doing with my life?

- You have to understand that your specific *purpose* for being here in this earth realm was authentically engineered by your Creator.

- You have to dedicate time for *prayer* and meditation so that you can connect with your ultimate source of authenticity – our Creator.

- You must know that it takes a great expanse of *energy* to live and maintain an authentic lifestyle. Thus, channeling your energies in the area of your original purpose becomes imperative.

- You must understand that whatever you *focus* on in life infuses your spirit, soul and body. Your focus should be on everything authentic in and around you in order to reproduce after that same order.

- You must grasp the important role that *priority* plays in manifesting an authentic life. Priority is the foundational wisdom for the allocation of time, energy and resources in discovering the anatomy of your authenticity.

- You must personally engage the phenomenon of *clarity* in order for your authentic streams to flow unhindered from within. Clear away the clutter from your life and allow the voice of clarity to speak to the authentic you.

- You must at all costs become intimately acquainted with your authentic *identity* as a person, that is, if you are going to reproduce the Creator's blue-print for your life. Identity is like a master-key for living an authentic life. Once possessed it provides unlimited access to the many doors of life.

- You have to know that once you make the internal shift to facilitate your mark of authenticity, the *trajectory* for your life will drastically be altered. You must be willing to make the necessary assessments and shifts in order to charter this new course.

- You have to gather the right *information,* if you are going to brand and sustain your authentic self. So many times we are informed but we are not rightly informed. Some of the paradigms we house due to inheritance, socialization or adaptation are not in alignment with our original purpose –this is the reason we are not getting original outcomes in life.

- You have to have a clear and just set of *values* when you are elevated into the realm of authenticity. The values you embrace and establish for governing yourself and everything which is connected to you, at this level, will foster healthy boundaries and bring balance to your life.

- You have to allow the essence of *creativity* to merge with the streams of authenticity on the inside of you. This union of creativity and authenticity becomes the birthing place for infinite possibilities relative to your life's assignment.

- You have to *forgive* and let go o*f the past,* and if it has to be revisited or referenced – let it serve as a tool of empowerment and a catalyst for the future. Forgive yourself and let go of past failures, bad judgment calls, investments betrayals, hurts, people, and misunderstandings. Give your authentic self a clean space to grow. As some people would say "wipe the slate clean and start all over again."

- You must b*e able t*o be *resilient, if you* are going to live authentically. You will experience some degree of hardship, resistance, misunderstandings and many other challenges which come with the territory. Understanding how to bounce back and be sustained becomes absolutely paramount.

- You have to understand it takes a great deal of *courage* to embrace your authenticity without allowing the external influences to dilute or shift you from the blue print for your life. Courage will cause you to become "pressure proof" against the many ideologies, suggestions and thoughts that are projected on you, which sometimes can cause you to question your authentic self and the path you're on.

- You have got to embrace this simple, yet profound phenomenon of *integrity.* Integrity means that you are a whole person – every facet of your triune being.

There is not a disparity with what you projected on the outside and what is actually going on the inside of you.

- You must be able to effectively facilitate the process of *character* development. It is said that "a good name is better than silver and gold." Your character is the embodiment of your authentic essence and reputation. You will be given many opportunities to build, refine and align you character to universal principles and patterns which will reflect the total nature and scope of the authentic you.

- You have to posture yourself to really work in *harmony* with everything and everyone around you, relative to accomplishing your authentic life's work. Working in harmony with all of the necessary resources around you to maximize your original potential eliminates envy, strife, sabotage, jealously, unhealthy-competition, and every other unhealthy latent proclivity of the human soul.

- You must *express* yourself authentically and boldly, within the context of healthy boundaries. The true expression of who you really are is not predicated upon external sources. Your uniqueness of expression as an individual hinges on your ability to know that you were created to manifest the highest and purest form of yourself on every plane of life.

I have given you some key fundamental time–tested principles which can help you. If you put them to work, they will work for you in helping you to discover the anatomy of your authenticity which is exactly what you were created to do, and the way you were created to uniquely express that specific work.

If you are going to embrace the anatomy of your authenticity, at all costs, you have to become intimately acquainted with some key fundamental principles and patterns that will incubate, accommodate and give birth to the "original you." The development and growth process can be much easier and clearer to navigate when these principles are in full operation. Once the aforementioned principles are embraced, understood and incorporated relative to your unique function here in this earth realm you will become an unstoppable force.

Embracing Your MARK of Authenticity
A Creed To Humanity

CHAPTER 5

The Enemies Of Your World of Authenticity

Enemies of Your State of Authenticity

There will always be opposing elements which will rise up to challenge you in your place of authenticity in life –beware and be aware of them!

Most people, after reading that statement will say "yesssssss" and immediately point outwards and not take the time to look within themselves. Many believe after all, it is everybody else's fault. We have been trained to only look for enemies from without! The simple truth of the matter is that there are enemies from both worlds working against your state of authenticity. Adversaries within and without…Let's take this journey together.

Imagine driving to work listening to your favorite radio station and suddenly the music was interrupted by this breaking news: "Terrorists just attacked and are holding several hundreds of people in one of our state buildings...there are no further details at this time." This of course, turned out to be one of the major conversational pieces of the work day, as everyone eagerly awaited an update on the state of affairs. Suppose you were driving on your way home and turned on your car radio only to hear that "The attack was aided from within." "The terrorists were only able to attack and hold individuals hostage because they had full cooperation from within." Or as most of us would say, "It was an inside job." One of the first thoughts that would flood the mind of people is 'Who would carry out such a devious act against their own people and why?'

Immediately, tons of analysts and specialists relative to this issue at hand would emerge and rush to the forefront of our televisions and radios everywhere to explore the dynamics of what happened and offer some kind of explanation to the people. Nonetheless, the same abiding questions would reside everywhere in the hearts and minds of people: "Who were the internal aiders and why did they enable such an attack on our state?" "What do the terrorists want?" "Will they let the hostages go?" "Will they kill them?" "What will become of this whole sadistic affair?"

What many of us are unaware of is that we all at some point in life have committed these very acts of attacks from within. Even though the example of terrorists being aided by inside intelligence, which in this case might be a bit extreme, the underlying and prevailing principles remain the same.

For so many of us, because of the corroded state of our world within, by default, we end up partnering with the enemies of the "state of authenticity" by allowing them to come in and wreak havoc in our lives. At this rate, any and everything from the outside can show up at any given point and enter our lives. However, the case maybe, you must know this one truth relative to your "internal world" and external activates: that adversarial projections or pressures from any external source are not nearly as powerful as a fortified and conscious world from within you. Everything on the inside of you will set the precedence for what is allowed to manifest on the outside of your life. Living without the awareness of the world of authenticity we inherently possess on the inside of us, consequently, will foster life without healthy boundaries.

It has been said that "knowledge is power." However, power becomes null and void if it is not properly understood and appropriated. If we are unaware of the operations of the many proverbial dynamics which are presented to us on a daily basis in our lives, when we decide to embrace our mark of authenticity, it will be very difficult to detect the measure of their workings in our lives.

Let's take a look at some of the most common enemies of your state of authenticity, both from within and without:

Where are your boundaries?

I was talking to a dear wise friend of mine some years ago, about how disillusioned and anguished I was with the state of life relative to dealing with some folks around me, and even in a broader sense in some cases. I remember saying to him "Why do people do stuff like that when it comes to me?" The whole time we were talking I noted he never really sympathized with me – he was somewhat silent the whole time. At the end of our conversation he said "Do me a favor." Then he began to tell me about a book on healthy boundaries and said, "Read it please." I immediately purchased the book and read it. I was then elevated to a new dimension of consciousness relative to governing my life. I quickly realized why he was silent the whole time when I was talking to him: I had been running my life like a country without a constitution or a city with limit. Can you imagine that? I had no healthy boundaries for my life. I was blaming everyone else when in actuality; I was my own worst enemy. What a state of affairs in which to find oneself. I was not even consciously aware of what was really being played out in my life.

This is really how many people live today and sadly enough; they blame everyone else for the condition in which they find themselves. They don't know that the consequences are simply a result of leading a life without boundaries. Your personal power and healthy boundaries are elaborate mechanisms set in motion to keep intruders out of your life, and also to guide you on your path in service to humanity. The nature and scope of your authentic life reside in the simple, yet timeless and powerful abiding principle of healthy boundaries for your life.

Sincere, but sincerely wrong:

Have you ever tolerated any unhealthy behavior(s) for so long that everyone around you sees this except you? That is because those behaviors have become so intertwined with who you are as a person that they have become second nature. This is one of the major intrinsic weapons used against so many today. Many people's intentions and motives could be as pure as ever, however, the practical application of these intentions and motives in life are far removed from the principles and patterns which will enable and reflect the essence of authentic living. How you are empowered as an individual and the services you offer to humanity have a meaningful and lasting impact. If this system of mal-adaptive behavior is not interrupted and altered in a positive manner, it could hurt you and others whom you are called to serve. You don't want to live in the realm of doing the right thing the wrong way because this could perpetually separate you from manifesting the full power of who you are authentically.

Identity theft:

Identity theft is on the rise, beware..! Many of us are walking around with a sense of lost identity. Somewhere along the course of life some of us have been "high jacked and held hostage" by someone else's opinion, judgment, ideology, and philosophy of us. We have allowed them to introduce us to an order that is counter-productive to our authentic self. This level of intrusion has affected so many people on so many levels, every day without them even realizing it. They do not have a working understanding of their own individuality and authenticity, so by default they give in to this kind of pressure from an external source. Identity truly comes from your original purpose. Your Purpose provides the authentic trajectory for your destiny.

The danger of dilution:

Dilution of the authentic self seems to be the norm of the day – almost like a common virus in today's society. Many of us find ourselves adapting to this form of living in order to flow in the common stream of things. In actuality, we were not created to flow just whenever or wherever, nor with whomever. We were created to stand out and allow the undiluted version of who we are to flow unto humanity from the innermost chambers of our authentic self. Sadly though, we always give so many pieces of who we are to our friends, family, loved-ones, associates and so many other voices who are vying for a space in our lives. This lack of self-preservation can sometimes remove us as far as the east is from the west, in relationship to our true purpose for being and our authentic essence for doing what we were assigned to do here in this lifetime.

Imagine buying a puzzle set that you are eagerly anticipating putting together, and some friends, family and other folks come over to your house and see the puzzle out on your coffee table. Each of them decided that they liked certain pieces of the puzzle so much that they all wanted to take their favorite pieces home. Without giving it a thought, you gave them permission to take the pieces that they all liked. When you were really ready to put the puzzle together to manifest the total scope of its hidden meaning, you soon realized that parts of the puzzle were missing because you gave them away. Now, the true intent and significance for buying the puzzle was realized! You could no longer enjoy the benefit putting the puzzle together, now that you have given them away. This is exactly what some of us do when we give away pieces of ourselves to the opinions, suggestions, personal beliefs, perceptions, and judgments of others; it dilutes the original version of our Creator's true intent for us as individuals.

The fear factor at play:

Fear, in my opinion is one of the "master captors" of individuals, prohibiting them from beholding, becoming and unleashing their authentic self in this lifetime!

People have so many forms of fears that they are yoked up with today: fear of venturing out, fear of the unknown and the future, fear of other people's opinions and criticisms, fear of the dark, fear of animals, fear of the past, fear of self-expression, fear of dying, fear of rejection and alienation, and a myriad of other forms of fear we see gripping the hearts of humanity from day to day. Some of us have partnered with the "fear factor" for so long that is has become a part of our life's anatomy. Fear has become rooted and grounded on the inside of us that in some instances, it is now chief governor of our lives.

When you transfer so much of your individual power to the "fear factor" you can never be delivered to a place of authentic living. There are countless number of individuals who have died with their dreams, desires, visions, and passions. They have allowed the "master captor" of fear to kidnap, hold, and sentence them to its prison for life. This phenomenon is equally as true for many of us who still breathe the breath of life. We live from day-to-day with the crippling and deadly emotion of fear without fully knowing that we are one breath away from freeing ourselves from its clutches. When fear is allowed to take preeminence in the space we are created to occupy, in our lives. It has a way of inviting its companions to move in as well: worry, insecurities, instability, and the list can be endless.

The "fear factor" is a key undercurrent for manifesting an inauthentic life: it speaks to you about everything that you would not be ever able to achieve. Conversely, when an individual conquers fear, this person is automatically ushered into a place where living authentically becomes an eternal possibility.

Let's play it safe:

So many of us embrace the "let's play it safe" factor – what I call "organized, sophisticated fear." We keep telling ourselves "I will play it safe in life always, I will never let myself go (think or come outside the box) to experience anything which will disappoint, challenge, stretch, discomfort, or let me down in life." Some like to say, "This is my comfort zone!" News flash! People, who incorporate this level of thinking automatically, have disqualified themselves from winning in life. The undercurrent of passivity will do only one thing for you, take you under and keep you under-developed relative to your created worth. You will never be able to enjoy the benefits of an authentic, powerful and thrilling life by remaining in the "let's play it in the safe zone."

We are designed to progressively transform into the person we really are every day. This process encompasses a wide range of life dynamics, failures, apprehensions, doubts, trials, triumphs, pain, grief, disappointments, wins and losses – just to say the least! This is just life, and life happens to all of us. No one is exempt from life's universal jurisdictions. However, we do get the awesome privilege of choosing our responses to life events which can ultimately lead us to creating the life we really want to lead, purely by choice...The power lies within our inherent ability to choose our path to purpose. When we respond to life by choosing our path to purpose, in spite of life's vicissitudes, there is no room for the *"let's play it safe factor"* to constrict, control or bind us to its limiting and crippling effects. We become a dynamic, unstoppable and unlimited force, relative to our life's authentic purpose.

Distorted Image:

The issue of a "distorted image" relative to individuals today can be safely categorized as one of the fastest global epidemics plaguing our human race. So many people have a very poor self-image. As a result, they wander through life's journey, looking on the outside at the many objectified images on TV, social media or where have you, as a point of reference for who they are. As I mentioned earlier in the book, "You are searching for yourself in all of the wrong places." The governing influence and the power of self-image, stems from the ability to understand your inherent authentic worth, when managed it in such a way, will reproduce after its kind in your external environment. People will respond to you according to the image you project, manage and brand. This is my working definition of a healthy self-image:

I -   **Imagine that you are the world's greatest**
M-   **Manage your emotions with healthy boundaries**
A -   **Activate your own gifts, talents, and abilities**
G-   **Greatness is already on the inside of you**
E-   **Empowered to live authentically every day**

Do not allow your own poor self-image to rob you from coming into contact with the "authentic you," which steers you to your place of original purpose in life. You have got to understand that the power of self-image will drive us to a place of achieving either favourable or unfavourable results in life. This is largely predicated on the imprints of our soul from life's journey, guided by our own belief of who we are. Let us first get the issue of our self–image together, then we will be able to sing the anthem of authenticity loudly and with boldness where ever we go.

The weight of external projections:

Many times these projections from the outside stem from other peoples own insecurities, jealously, fears, internal struggles, and in some case a lack of knowing who they are as an authentic creation. Nonetheless, if you do not understand how this particular "enemy" of authenticity works, you will, in many instances take on false burdens, which will keep you yoked up to the projections of other people.

Have you ever had anyone to project anything on you? Maybe you thought for a split second it was something from your own soul and in that very split second you realized that it wasn't you after all, but it emanated from the realm of that individual's soul. You have to be on the lookout for this one, "external projections," it is a "biggie!" Many people deal with these every day. They buckle under the weight of external projections without realizing what is really going on in their world. When you are resolute about living your life authentically, you have to learn how to accentuate the areas of your gifting and also be aware of, and manage your weakness. So, when someone shows up in your life with their own ideas and perceptions of who you are as an individual and project something on you, out of their own beliefs, you are able to recognize it, at a moment's notice.

They are on the attack:

It would be a great injustice for me not to warn you that once you have resigned to place of living your life authentically, it will be tested. So many forces will rise up and assign themselves to challenge that resolve. Some people will outright oppose everything you do; others will criticize, gossip, attempt to malign your character and pass all kinds of judgments. Some may even go the lengths to sabotage projects and movements that have been birthed by you, or of which you are a part. You should never allow any unhealthy outside force to influence and adjust the path of your original life's assignment.

It is highly imperative to recognize these tactics and strategies, and at the same time remain unshakable with your resolve to continue allowing the undercurrent of authenticity to influence the temperature of your internal and external environment.

Birth rights sold:

It is *your **inalienable right*** to activate and brand your authentic worth as an individual. However, tons of people abdicate the place in which they were meant to reign in life. This is what I refer to as "selling your birth rights" to circumstances and in some instances people. This phenomenon is a constant "life sore" for humanity. Many individuals give up on themselves too easily. Sometimes, because of a lack of resources, support, validation, understanding, motivation, discipline, knowledge, and just simply the courage to become that authentic person and live in the authentic space they were created to occupy.

Once the anatomy of your authenticity is compromised, by your own volition, it has a rippling effect in every area of your life. Remember, earlier in the book I talked about whatever you host internally as an individual, whether, it is erroneous or in alignment with universal principles and patterns, will reproduce itself in your immediate atmosphere? So, if you walk away from who you really are as person, you disconnect yourself from everything and everyone that has been set in motion to facilitate your life's purpose.

The great power struggle:

When I speak of the power struggle in this context, I am referring to your personal power, over which you are stewards. The power struggle continues every day, as we endeavor to make sense out of why we give away so much of ourselves. This sometimes lands us in a place of disillusionment, anguish, pain, discouragement, and brokenness. Note carefully, I am not referring to giving away yourself in service to humanity, which should be largely governed by healthy boundaries. I am specifically dealing with the issues of giving up so much of your personal power to sources incongruent to your anatomy of authenticity, that it causes you to live in a place of conflict and struggle with your personal power. How much of ourselves do we give away, and still not lose ourselves in the matrix?

You ask yourself the same questions in silence. Why can't I just say no or not now to people? Why do I always end up with the short end of the stick? Why do I engage in activities with myself or individuals that I know to my core are unhealthy for me but I just can't seem to stop?

This is the simple truth: you have to become personally acquainted with the "taking back your personal power concept", coupled with personal responsibility. You have to decide the balance of the power equation for your life by asking yourself what dimension of power you are willing to give away in the context of healthy boundaries and to what degree you will reserve for yourself. This way you can neutralize the effects of the "power struggle" in your life and foster an environment which will promote balance, wisdom, healthy-boundaries and authenticity.

These enemies of your authenticity mentioned above are by no means exclusive to the list. I am pretty sure after reading this chapter you have started compiling a list for yourself. Moreover, these concepts are not highlighted for you to be thrown into hyper–vigilance mode, or to take on a proverbial posture towards yourself or others.   As you continually progress on your authentic trajectory you must become aware of the many forms of intrinsic and extrinsic weapons which can sabotage the natural progression of your authentic state. This keen awareness will establish you at a vantage point, enabling you to enjoy the holistic benefits of authenticity. You will then become empowered to facilitate the following in your life:

- **Be in charge of charting the course for your life without excuses**
- **Cultivate and sustain an environment for growth, development, resilience, purpose and authenticity**

- **Be a personal architect for your individual purpose while helping others as well**
- **Confront and resolve the real life issues that we often repress, suppress and sweep under the rug**
- **Be free from any internal clutter and proclivities which can override your authentic purpose in an unhealthy way**
- **Create a sustainable movement in your immediate environment, which will perpetually steer you in the direction of your authentic life work, giving yourself away in service to humanity.**

This level of knowledge and understanding, with regard to the enemies of your authenticity, will incubate your longevity in the business of authentic living. You will have no choice but to become consciously involved with the processes of life, in spite of its multi–dimensional challenges which attend our path every day.

Embracing Your Mark of Authenticity

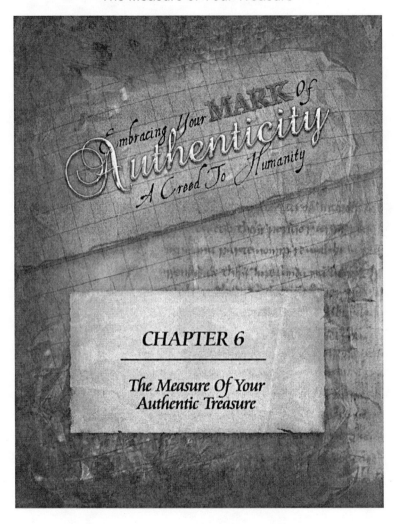

Embracing Your MARK *of*
Authenticity
A Creed To Humanity

CHAPTER 6

The Measure Of Your
Authentic Treasure

Embracing Your Mark of Authenticity

The Measure of Your Treasure

The Mark of Your Authenticity is purely engraved on your life by the measure of your treasure, look no further!

Throughout this book, my constant emphasis of this principle, that you are the *"highest and most valuable investment of the Creator in this earth realm",* is not to bore you, it is simply because I want you to become intimately involved with this powerful and life transforming concept, your *authentic worth* here in this lifetime. The other important piece of the puzzle is for you to have a working understanding of the measure of your own treasure, which will empower you to live an authentic life. For so many of us, the outward proverbial chases for "worth and possessions" become the motto of our lives. The sad reality is that the more relentless the pursuits are, the more we end up losing ourselves in the process. *You are who you are really looking for!*

I believe all of us who are caught up in this perpetual cycle of looking on the outside for what has already been invested on the inside should ask ourselves a question. This

87

is the exact same question I asked myself some years ago: "Why am I searching for myself in all of the wrong places?" It's not that the quest for your treasure is illegitimate, but when our intent is misguided and the search for authenticity is in question, we end up violating Universal principles and patterns which can cause harm to ourselves and others. We end up diluting the true intent and essence of service to one another and humanity as a whole.

here is the proof of your message? I remember I was invited to speak at a particular forum when I was very young, impressionable and had a lot to say on the subject matter of "purpose." At the end of my teaching, I was asked the following by one of the leaders: "Where is the proof of your message? You do not have the 'material things' to show for what you were teaching." I had an idea about where the question was heading, but I wanted to make it clear that I understood what "proof of purpose" meant to the leader who asked me that question. I realized in that moment a lot of us judge people and their success of purpose based on material trappings. How many of us allow the opinions, judgments of other people and their interpretation of purpose to affect the way we see ourselves? Consequently, if we are not awakened to the true understanding of who we are and what has already been deposited on the inside of us to accomplish our life's work, we will begin the illusive journey towards 'the stuff' to prove that we are successful by society's standards.

There is a relentless quest, by individuals for external sources to validate "the measure of their treasure" in today's world. More and more people are searching for that one moment, that place, person or thing to give them some kind of significance or meaning in life. To many individuals, all of the material trapping on the outside that can be measured by this three dimensional world in which we live constitute purpose. It may be a house, car, some money in the bank, maybe a position or title and sometimes even our associations in some instances. Unfortunately, some acquire all of the things according to society's standards of success in an effort to authenticate their life's purpose. Yet, at the end of the day there is still a void on the inside of many such individuals. They still have not found themselves and the ability to connect with and live from that place of authenticity still remains untapped.

The proof of your authentic purpose shows up in the "measure of your treasure" which is on the inside of you – never doubt that. Let's go on a journey right now to discover "Where is the proof of your purpose."

The nature and scope of your treasure on the inside should be a proportionate reflection of the authentic work you were designed for. The "measure of your treasure" includes your specific personality, gifts, talents, and abilities, which were deliberately invested on the inside of you by your Creator. You are wired to discover, cultivate and utilize your treasures within in you in accordance with the essence of your authenticity. The discovery and utilization of your unique gifts and talents congruent to your purpose will ultimately provide for you on every level and catapult you to your place of destiny.

However, the appropriation of your life's purpose must be understood within the context of "Seedtime and Harvest." Whatever you sow you will reap. This principle is one of the surest Universal principles created and set in motion by the Creator to ensure our personal discovery and establishment of purpose; that is, without violating ourselves and others.

One of the ills of society today is that a lot of people look at some individuals who seemly "have it together" and they are automatically ushered into a realm of greed, envy and jealously. They want that same life for themselves without sowing the necessary seeds to ensure a harvest down the road. These individuals do not want to be a personal steward over their own lives, nor do they stop to understand that those seemingly successful people have applied and still are applying certain life principles and strategies to get to where they are in life.

One of the things I learned from Social Studies, Political Science and History class, is that whenever a great kingdom, nation or civilization is born, one of the first things government and leaders establish is an authentic vision for that nation. It is hard to succeed without developing a written plan for success.

The next order of business is to assess what natural and human resources we have on board in order to operationalize the original vision. This principle holds true with us as individuals from the day we were born – given life by our Creator. He had a distinctive purpose for you in mind and He invested a measure of treasure on the inside of you. The unique gifts, talents, and abilities are one of the key indicators that you are more than just a day–to–day existence. That's proof enough that you are an all-time "one of a kind" specimen in the universe.

The measure of your treasure on the inside of you spans wide and deep. The Creator has invested a measure of His Treasure on the inside of you and because He is, you are. It is as simple as that. Right now, as you read this book, you must realize that you are more than equipped to identify, embrace, develop and live an authentic life. Let's open up your treasure box to see what we can find. You can use these treasures to facilitate your authentic journey.

There are so many dimensions to who you are as an individual, which will ultimately contribute to the "measure of your treasure" enameling the full scope of authenticity in your life.

Your Mind:

This is one of the greatest treasures you will ever possess – your mind. I like to refer to the mind as the central processing unit of the soul. It houses all of your thought life. It is with the mind's eye that we are able to perceive the authentic life we are called to lead. The trajectory of that authentic life will ultimately be controlled by the measure of your mind. Whatever you meditate upon will infuse your being: sprit, soul and body. The object of your meditation will take on a life of its own and will manifest in your world. Let's manage our thoughts in accordance with our original life's assignment.

Your Will:

The chief decision maker of our being is our will. It is one of the major determining factors relative to living an authentic life. Decisions! Decisions! Decisions! We all make them, and we all don't make them. Your will is one of the major ports of entry to your life. Whatever you let in and whatever you let out is all an act of your own will. It's that important and inextricability connected to living an original life.

The right to your own will, congruent to an authentic life is a divine provision afforded you by your Creator. Many people do not understand this concept and they give away their will power to other people, places, and things, rendering themselves powerless. The secret of really living and sustaining an authentic life lies in the ability to make well-informed decisions that will steer you to the place of your life's ultimate purpose. The faculty of your will gives way to the full "measure of your treasure" when embracing an authentic life. The will is the decision maker of the soul, - these simple expressions: **yes, no, maybe, not now, let me think about it or I am not sure,** all flow from your will.

Your Heart:

The heart is the center of your treasure and your soul; your belief s system. It is from the dimension of the heart that life really emanates. If you are ever going to perceive, conceive, and achieve an authentic life it will be from the faculty of the heart. Everything that we value, our morals, ethics, manners, world views, ideologies and philosophies flow from the mainstream of our existence - the heart. Your heart is one of the highest and most powerful compartments of your soul, and it affords you the opportunity of manifesting your authentic self. Remember those dreams and visions you had growing up that you pondered in your heart? To you, they were so surreal.

Whenever you had those impressions you were so sure that was who you really were or wanted to be. Silently you kind of memorialized those dreams and visions and did not share them with anyone because they would think you were crazy or too daring. Well, it was the heart the enabled you to experience and archive those impressions. This is how important the heart is in relation to our authentic existence. Even when the vicissitudes of life attempt to choke out those dreams, visions and impressions, if we dig hard and long enough, we will find them right there in our hearts

Your Emotions:

This is the thermostat and scale of your soul. It checks the temperature and brings balance to the "measure of your treasure." Hence, this is a very critical and key component to developing an authentic lifestyle. If you fully understand the purpose and power of your emotions as it relates to authenticity, you will begin to utilize this information to your advantage. The faculty of your emotions enables you connect with your authentic feelings. If you really pay attention to your innermost feelings without repressing or suppressing them, you will always have a working understanding of what's going on with your inner world. You will also be able to make sense of a lot of relational issues you face with other people on a daily basis.

Your emotions facilitate the intangibles and the unquantifiable in life. It is from this dimension that we love or hate, feel happy or sad, feel joy or grief, pain or wellness. The quality of energy emitted in our immediate atmosphere and world at large is filtered by our emotions. This is how intricately connected our emotions are to our every fiber of living an authentic life.

Gifts, Talents and Abilities:

You are never left without the resources to accommodate your authentic life's work. Your gifts, talents and abilities are the perfect indicators. Do you recall anyone saying to you "You are just a natural at that" or "You should really consider being X or Y, you are just so good at that?" Those were you gifts in operation. They are already on the inside of you. Sadly, most people go through life ignoring their gifts and areas of their greatest influence. Yet they ask themselves from day-to-day, "Why on God's earth, am I here?"

Your individual gifts, talents and abilities are the currency for appropriating an authentic life. Gifting and authenticity are never separated variables relative to you fulfilling your destiny. The two are eternally woven together. Why is this so? The unique gifting and talents which you possess are meant to authenticate and validate your life's purpose.

Embracing Your Mark of Authenticity

Deep down in the reservoir of your treasures are so many undiscovered gifts, talents, and abilities. I believe life lessons provide so many opportunities for us to manifest our treasures but so many are pre-occupied with the mundane trappings of: life, working, cooking, cleaning the house, paying the bills, raising the kids, attending school, grocery shopping, washing the car ,eating sleeping, and waking up. It's not that any of those things are not essential, but when you ignore a true opportunity to nurture and utilize your gifts to ensure an authentic life, sooner or later you wind up disenchanted at some point in life.

Even though we can possess many gifts, talents, and abilities – I earnestly believe there is a dominant one that you possess, which is your strongest point of influence; that one dominant trait that will cause you to sit comfortably in the seat of your purpose. This realization will steer you to the highest point of your authentic self.

Your Essence:

The essence of anything lights up a room or influences the fragrance of the atmosphere. It brings an element of distinction to a person, place or thing. This is exactly the reason you were given your unique authentic essence - to bring a unique flavor to life which was not present before. The essence of who you are as an individual is one of the most important components of the "measure of your treasure" on the inside of you. It holds the fabric of the anatomy of your authenticity together. It gives you an opportunity to really present your original flavor to society without trying to duplicate someone else's style.

Many have not discovered this key ingredient for their authentic lives as yet. As a result, they fall into to the trap of wanting to do "it" just like the other people. Many times we find ourselves saying, "I wanna or got to do it just like him or her – they just know how to do this or that so well." The truth of the matter is those people that possess an undiluted essence and reputation that is congruent to their original life's purpose discovered the secret a long ago. They have allowed their own flavor, style, swag, essence, and passion to emerge from deep within to serve themselves and others well.

You have the same inherent mechanism within you to allow your essence of authenticity to break forth on every level of your life. Remember, you will be known for the unique flavor you bring to life's table.

Your Vision:

Vision! Vision! Vision! It is the driving force of really living an authentic life. It is the single most important "measure of your treasure" which you possess. Without a vision for your life, you can forget the whole notion of authentic living. Vision is another master key for activating an authentic trajectory for your life. If it is not clear and tailored to your goals, aims, objectives, desires, passion, mission, and purpose, you will end up wherever the tides of life take you.

I believe every single human being possesses a vision deep within, whether they realize it or not - It is just an inalienable provision, afforded us by our Creator. It is also my heart-felt view that the "God invested vision" for your life, authenticates your very existence. Your vision is right there sitting on the inside of you. It is waiting to be identified, embraced, developed, and unleashed. When vision is clearly defined by you, it serves as a portrait reminder of what the blueprint for your life looks like. It helps you to look back at your life and say, "This is where I was." It also enables you to accurately assess where you are currently relative to your life's mission. Your vision will also function as a catalyst for the future. Vision will capture the total scope of your authentic assignment. It stands as a beacon from within, and it also provides a clear signal to those around you concerning where you are and where you would like to go.

Before you even go on to the next chapter of this book, stop and either formulate or revisit your life vision.

Your Ideas and Thoughts:

Have you ever turned on the television or listened to the radio and you see the same idea you have had for a long time but never acted on it? Your thoughts and ideas are probably your greatest intellectual property you will ever possess. Thoughts and ideas are already tangible things and even at the moment they are conceived, they can be achieved by you with some effort. Think for a moment about the things you see, use and buy everyday…at some point all of these things existed in the realm of somebody's mind as a thought. The difference between many of us and those individuals who were able to move a thought from conceptualization to operationalization is they acted on them.

You have so many creative ideas and original thoughts flowing to you and through you right now, even as you are reading this book. Many of the environments a lot of us were raised in did not encourage our creative ideas and authentic expression of thought. Every time we attempted to share our thoughts and ideas, we were either laughed at, told to stop dreaming, or we were avoided or totally ignored.

The thoughts and ideas of many individuals have transformed the world we live in today. The concepts that originated from some of these great minds, have inspired inventors to create what we see manifested today in physical and tangible forms. For instance, the computer, the car, the washing machine, the toaster, the electric or gas stove, the pen, and cell phone, just to mention a few. You should place a high premium on your original thoughts and your creative ideas. You never know the transforming power they hold and how much they can change the course of history. The very thought and idea on the back-burner of your mind can be the very thought which may introduce you to the globe. Take Bill Gates for example, the inventor of the Microsoft program. He is known throughout the world and is a household name because of his invention.

Our thought life is the true "life" of the authentic trademark placed on us from the day we were born. We must endeavor to cultivate it in such a way until we are transformed into our authentic self.

Your Capacity:

The natural inherent ability which insulates, contains, and maintains your vision pertaining to your authentic life's work. This is your capacity. You are created to capacitate everything which you will ever set out to accomplish in line with your original life's function. Capacity is the dimension which brings the total scope of the "measure of your treasure" to life.

One of the most important factors we have to understand when embracing our authenticity is that everything has to be measured in the context of reality. Although I believe that perception plays a key role in shaping our realities, we have to be practical and honest with our evaluation of ourselves at the same token. You don't want to align yourself to an assignment that you were never meant to accomplish.

It is one thing for you to know from the inner most recesses of your being that you are wired for something great, in addition to knowing you have the capacity to facilitate that work, but you might be misappropriating certain principles relative to making that vision for your life tangible. In this case, that way you can always go back to the drawing board, and keep re-evaluating what you are doing wrong relative to your vision. It is also possible that you could be doing all the right things; however, it may not be the season for full manifestation of that vision.

With the same breath, it is a totally different scenario for you keep trying to accomplish something for which you do not have the capacity. In this case, nothing about you is wired for what you are hoping to achieve. What you are trying to do goes against the very core of who you were created to be. In some cases, if what we are striving for is finally achieved there is no gratification and true purpose to it. I am firmly of the view that every person has an authentic office to occupy and the built-in capacity to own that space. When your authentic purpose is realized, your capacity for that purpose will be maximized. Get familiar with your capacity – the length, breath, height, and depth of who you really are. Always be honest with yourself; it's only then that you can give way to the total scope of your authentic life's assignment.

Your Creativity:

We were created to be creators, make no mistake about that. From the way we fix our hair, houses, the buildings we build with the intricate architectural designs, the way we dress ourselves up, even the way Even the way I will be designing this book cover after I am finished writing it. These are all creative expressions of who we really are. Creativity is the chief driving force behind the mark of distinction that you have or will be known for. Deep down on the inside of all of us is that creative spark. This spark needs igniting in order to see the true fruits of authentic living.

The creativity and authenticity on the inside of you are as compatible as wet and water; once you have made a decision to embrace your mark of authenticity, creativity will emerge from the inside of you like a well spring. It is creativity that has inspired a standard of living that says the mundane and ordinary just will not do in life. In this age we are living in, where everything is market-driven, it is not enough to land the competition; you have to be able to bring an unusual dimension of creativity to the market with a creative edge. This phenomenon holds true as well for our own lives, if understood in its proper context. Every individual has a creative edge to bring to the table that can make an impression to others, irrespective of where you are on life's continuum.

Your Imagination:

Your imagination is powerful beyond measure: it is the single most underestimated dimension of our existence. It engages insight and foresight that can lead us to our authentic destiny. One of the most amazing features of our imagination is that it captures images of our desires, goals, dreams and visions. I know for sure that you have experienced the benefits of your imagination at some point or the other. How about that dream home, car, job, spouse, pay, and clothes? Sometimes we even imagine ourselves acting, speaking, singing and so many other things which we dearly hope for and visualize for our lives. Many times we wind up saying to ourselves "This is all just a figment of my imagination, it will never happen."

Most of us are not aware of how powerful our imagination is but if it's used correctly, it will empower us to capture, incubate and give birth in the physical world what we envisioned in the unseen world. Our imagination is very much real and is an integral part of the anatomy of our authentic lives. One of the things which really fascinates me about our imaginations is that we enter that realm uninterrupted and uncensored by anyone else. We make the journey there alone and it is a very personal and private endeavor.

We should allow our Creator to impress us through the use of our imagination. All of His investments in us visit us from time-to-time in the realm of our imagination as a reminder to let us know these tools are waiting to manifest in our lives.

Your Perception:

Your perception is the eye of your belief system or your heart as we know it. I also like to refer to perception as the lenses of life. When you enable the full application of your original self-manifesting, you can really utilize the power of your perception to bring into focus your authentic life course.

The Measure of Your Treasure

It is said by many that "your perception is your reality." However, it is my view that perception is far more powerful than a basis of reality, on my assessment of this notion. I pose this view because reality is manifested by the thoughts we perceive and conceive; it is never the other way around, where perception is controlled by reality. You can easily adjust your thoughts and perceptions and a new reality will be born based on that adjustment - Yes, you can literally change your thoughts in order to change your life.

What happens, to many of us throughout the course of our lives, is those vicissitudes begin to tarnish the purity of our perception. When we should be using the power of our perception to our advantage, we find ourselves in the place of disillusionment and jaded at life, all because we are not allowing our perceptions to produce the kind of force, which will generate the kind of life we want to experience.

This is largely because there is usually a clogging or clutter somewhere in our lives that is preventing us from manifesting the full intent and expression of our authenticity. These are some of the unsightly impressions we pick up along the way through the lenses of our life (our perception): guilt, shame, rage, worry, unforgiveness, doubt, malice, anger, confusion, envy, and fear – just to mention a few. We need to get rid of all of the aforementioned, which induces stagnation to our authentic self. We must begin to use the purity of our perception to harness the power of authentic living.

<u>Your Appetite:</u>

Your appetite for the things of life is the master-mind behind your passion and drive for living an authentic life. This is the reason you should invest a considerable amount of time and energy feeding yourself with all of the necessary stimuli for creating an authentic environment.

This unique dimension of our existence (our appetite) develops our distinct thirst and flavor for life. Every single authentic dream, vision, desire, imagination, goal, passion, and desire emanates from the realm of your appetite.

Your Experiences:

Your experiences could be a great teacher and asset, if you respond to life lessons with the proper perspective. I am sure you have heard this saying: "Live and learn." I will take it a step further...live, learn, and leap into your future. If you sit back and reflect on the things that you have accrued, the good, the bad, the ugly, the highs, the lows, the victories, and the defects, your experiences can be used to shape the sphere of your authenticity. The one thing we can all conclude is that no human being is exempt from the variations of life. Everything we experience is simply the nature of living in this earth realm.

You can use everything you have experienced up until this point of your life, with the proper perspective to your advantage. Some people are stuck by saying "I have been through so much in life" and their story ends there. Why not say "I have been through so much in life, but what can I learn from my life experiences?"

You are the measure of your treasure, which is already invested on the inside of you!

In the prior chapters, I have opened you up to a multi-faceted you - the many dimensions of who you are already. It is my sincere desire that by now you have captured the "measure of your treasure." Whatever posture you find yourself in while reading this book, I'm sure you are already thinking about how you will ignite and integrate those different parts of your authentic make-up to brand the true essence of who you are. Don't spend another day saying to yourself, "I am nothing or nobody and I have nothing to offer anyone, or bring to life's table" or, I will never amount to anything." The next time you or someone else tries to reduce you beneath your authentic worth, take out a pen or pencil and write this down: ***"I am the measure of my treasure, which is already invested on the inside of me."*** Next, list the different treasures (the ones I gave you and even the ones you can come up with) and say them out aloud to affirm yourself and conform yourself according to your authentic worth. This simple exercise will reconfigure your atmosphere with the currents of authenticity and your true identity. Before you know it, you will have aligned yourself closer to all of the resources you have and will need to fulfill your destiny.

I want to drop a quick line to those of you who might not be battling with the "I am nothing, I am nobody", or just scarching for yourself. You are seemly established and comfortable with whatever you are doing. And you know to the core of your being that what you are doing and how you are doing it, do not resonate with the fibers of your authentic being. Stop, think, and consider the invitation to the realm of authenticity. It's not about what we do and how much we acquire along the journey of life: it is really underscoring all of what we do with the mark of authenticity.

CHAPTER 7

*The Source And Power
Of Your Authenticity*

The Source and Power of your authenticity

The source of our authenticity is powerful, and that power source is the Creator - the Creator of the Universe.

Think for a moment about everything which is created precisely and intelligently, everything working in concert to support its Creator's master plan for its existence: The galaxies, moon, sun, stars, oceans, and the earth ever functioning in accordance with divine principles and patterns of order. None of these entities ask for their nature of authenticity on a daily basis in order to exist – they are just aligned to the source and power of their existence and functioning in harmony with Mother Nature. This is exactly how we should function as individuals – being fully plugged into our source and power of our set place of authenticity in earth realm...*THE CREATOR HIMSELF!*

The Source and Power of your Authenticity

The Sun does not rise one day and decide it wants to be the Moon. Neither does the Ocean say to the Earth, "Cease to exist in your original place and take my place and I will take yours." Absolutely not - all of these created elements are positioned majestically, individually and authentically, and are postured that way eternally. **For the rest of your life, never raise the question about whether or not you have what it takes to live an authentic life. Just accept this simple truth, that your mark or print is one in approximately seven billion. Yes, your mark will never be duplicated in this life time or the one to come.**

Look at this intricate yet simple enough principle; creation in all its majesty, splendor, and unique design is aligned to its authentic source of power. Therefore, as human beings, and the crown of creation; when we align ourselves to the source and power of our authenticity, the radiating principle of which we are created to be will reproduce itself. The "real you" will extend to your immediate environment and will flow to the world at large. **Then and only then will people come to know the undiluted version of who you are really created to be.**

I have come to learn a very simple but astounding principle, which is, there is always an undercurrent to what's currently playing out in my life. This principle drives me to a desired end on a constant basis. Whatever occupies the gates and doors of your soul (your heart, your will, your emotions, your mind) will generate that very quality of energy and drive in your life to produce after its kind. Your vision, aims, objectives, passions, dreams, desires, mission and goals are all upheld by this guiding principle – the undercurrent or pillars of your belief system flow into every area and on every level of your life.

What and who is your power source of your life?

Have you allowed a pulse and heartbeat of external sources or forces to dictate to you what authenticity is for you? Are you living out the desires of others who introduced some concept, thought or idea to you years ago? Are you trying tirelessly to force something that does not fit your life? Have you made decisions relative to life because you just had to and did not really want to? Can you honestly answer the previous questions without the influences of any external sources and forces? By whose convictions are you living? If you interviewed yourself for a heart-felt and uncensored answer, what would your answer(s) be?

I believe only you and the source and power of your authenticity - your Creator, hold the key to unlock the prison doors to set you free from an unfulfilled and inauthentic life. No one else and nothing else can give a more accurate and detailed description of the measures of who you really are. Partnering with your power source to unleash a "one in approximately seven billion you" will perpetually deliver you to a place of beholding and becoming your authentic self. Let me just be crystal clear for a quick second. When I speak of self, I am not referring to selfishness, narcissism or their affiliates. I am alluding to you as an individual, a distinctive and authentic created expression of your Creator.

The purpose of your power source:

The Source and Power of your authenticity will ignite, inspire, invigorate, empower, and sustain you on the road of your life's work. It will also serve as the Chief Pillar for the purpose of "your being and the reason for your doing."

The balance of power phenomenon:

The balance of power index relative to your authentic life's work, will afford you the opportunity of discovering your mark of authenticity - I charge you to find it, own it, brand it and serve it. The process of branding who you are and how you serve it to humanity will enable you to understand that you were never given the gift of authenticity to serve yourself, win trophies or awards; authenticity was given to you to be of service to humanity.

All of the signs are there:

Some people might say "Well I don't know what my mark of authenticity is, much less how to be plugged into the power source of that mark." The truth is that you have not invested the time to find out who you really are. Don't look anywhere else other than within the burning desires of your heart. Every so often, through life lessons, we are given an opportunity to recolonize that mark. The mark of authenticity is never separated from your inherent God-given abilities, whether dominant or dormant gifts and talents. All of what you were born with to support your desire for an authentic life speaks to you every day in the form of experiences and opportunities. My question to you is, "Are you listening and are you paying attention to all of the signs and symptoms, which are always manifesting just within the horizon of your everyday life?" These signs give a good indication of your mark of authenticity.

Charge your life with currents of authenticity:

One of the most significant ways of powering up and charging your life with the currents of authenticity is by managing the undercurrents of your soul. Your will, heart, mind and emotions must work together as a well-oiled machine in order to reflect the true essence of your authentic nature in your external environment. Everything which springs forth from the dimensions of your soul will produce the quality focus, energy and consecration that will perpetually sustain you in your place of authenticity.

Seedtime and harvest:

The law of authenticity embodies a very powerful principle of progression and promotion relative to that specific mark you inherently possess. You don't have to stump, walk, or violate any of life's eternal patterns to find your way into your place of success and originality. Our Creator has created and established universal principles, patterns and laws to ensure our personal success and advancement relative to our authentic life assignment.

The real and the ideal:

So many people are caught up and held hostage by the whole thought of projecting an ideal image to the public, because that is just the way society is fashioned nowadays to respond to people and life issues at large. For many people, it's all about the glitz, glamour, gold, and the glory, even if it is at the expense of their own authenticity. When you make the decision to really live in your own skin, you don't have to buckle under to the pressures of life that will take you away from your original function. You will naturally progress at a rate and by principles which allow you to become more and more of who you were meant to be. This of course would eliminate the possibility of you wearing any mask to protect yourself.

Rites of passage:

As humans we are inherently wired to respond to any and everything authentic. People everywhere are looking for the next authentic thought, idea, or person. They are really tired of the "wannabe's", and widespread duplication of someone or something else that they have had or seen before. Will you accept the challenge of eliminating this global shortage? One of the basic fundamentals and power of authentic living is the rites of passage you are afforded throughout life's gates. Think for a moment about the whole purpose of someone being granted the "rites of passage." When that happens, the person is perpetually commissioned and thrust into a realm of authenticity whereby he or she is now legitimately able to function on every level in that place of unlimited access.

Patience in the pot:

When we decide to embrace our mark of authenticity, one of the virtues we really have to come to grips with and manage in today's world is *patience*. This seems to be the missing ingredient from the menu of life. Seemingly, everybody wants to be the other person, or have what they have. Everybody wants to be the next "big thing" or be in the lime light of life. Now, understand what I am trying to say here for a minute. Nothing is wrong with wanting to express the fullness of what you believe your Creator has invested in you as an individual. However, patience must be the key ingredient in the process of identifying and manifesting your authentic self. You should never allow anyone to make you feel bad or guilty for wanting more out of life. However, it becomes an issue when you want from life something you have not prepared for or invested in, just so you can expect a propitious return.

The power chair:

The power and nature of authenticity will ultimately steer and land you comfortably in the seat of your purpose, without you having to compromise to be recognized. When this posture is assumed as you mature through the journey of life, and you are embracing who you are authentically, you are better able to celebrate others in their place of assignment in life without diminishing who you are as a person. The essence and nature of harmony and celebration come alive in this instance to create a wonderful synthesis of true service to humanity.

The nooses of yesterday:

If you constantly magnify all of the negativity of yesterday you will never have any energy to expend towards today and a greater hope for tomorrow. The source and power of your authenticity will never be accentuated in your life if you keep allowing the stings of yesterday to hold you hostage and ultimately define who you are as a person. My philosophy relative to this is live, evaluate, learn, and leap into the newness of today and endless possibilities for tomorrow. The essence and newness of today ultimately sets the trajectory for tomorrow. This creates a new movement in our lives…catapulting us into a favorable place, all predicated on our decision and willingness to detach from the old unwanted cycles of yesterday.

The bold and the beautiful factor:

Being **"bold and beautiful"** is a rare commodity these days, because most people aren't being their authentic self. They carry around a sense of insignificance and unfulfillment. When you have truly discovered who and what you are called to do in life, you embrace it, and you find an original way to brand and serve it to humanity. There should be no "shame in your game" when you have arisen to the occasion of embracing your mark of authenticity and are undergirded by its true source and power. Rather, you become bold and beautiful. There will always be a level of confidence, humility and assurance which will undergird you, when you set out to accomplish anything.

===

Power it up, turn it up and live it up!

I believe unequivocally that when we grasp this concept of being aligned to our power source and our term of reference for living an authentic life are clarified; we will be unstoppable because we will be guided by the power and principles of authenticity. It will only be a matter of time before you are waking up every day with great joy and anticipation of what that day will bring you. All of the tangibles relative to your dreams, vision, passions, desires, needs and wants (the true essence of your life's purpose) will begin to reproduce themselves in your immediate environment. This will however, depend on your willingness to understand and activate the power and principles of authentic living.

I firmly believe that more and more we will begin to experience a myriad of multi-dimensional expressions of authenticity on every level across the globe. People are tired of living in the shadows of someone else, or being handled as an afterthought by others in society. Shock waves upon shock waves of authenticity will emerge and consequently be disseminated throughout the world. My challenge to you as a reader of this book is simply this:

don't sit, read and not activate the principles you have learned or the principles that were just simply reinforced as a result of reading this book. Get involved right where you are now. Get other people involved and start a movement in your immediate environment which will eventually sustain itself and affect and ignite other individuals to do the same. People can and will only respond to the degree of understanding you have of your authentic self. When you truly understand and embrace this truth, you will literally shift the currents in your life to a place of satisfaction and significance.

Every person is called to attention to embrace this powerful, timeless and distinctive mark on their individual lives, the mark of authenticity in a powerful fashion-do not ignore this challenge. Do not allow time to pass you by, sitting somewhere or doing nothing, feeling unsatisfied with the state of your life – wishing you had embarked on your desired journey of an authentic life. You are in the right place at the right time reading this book, and you are ready to lead a powerful, significant, organic and flavorful life. *Remember this,* **the source of our authenticity is powerful, and that power source is the Creator of the universe. You are never without the power you need** and want to live an authentic life. Inherently, we are all created to simultaneously embrace the mark and travel the path of authenticity.

Embracing Your Mark of Authenticity

Embracing Your MARK of Authenticity
A Creed To Humanity

CHAPTER 8

An Authentic Constellation

An Authentic Constellation

Authentic Minds Converge

I have deliberately opening up this chapter and called it "An Authentic Constellation – The Meeting of the Minds". This section contains varying viewpoints of individuals from a variety of backgrounds. These individuals have been socialized on diametrically opposite paths and have all formulated their personal world view on authenticity. The whole aim of this effort was to have the contributors reach down into the depths of who they really are as uniquely created individuals and explain what authenticity means to them. The Meeting begins:

This, I know, is true: The best way to help (and inspire) other people is to be my authentic self. What, and who, is my authentic self? When I am unafraid to speak from my deepest heart; when I am fearful of my darkest thoughts, and think through them, and reconcile them, and share them anyway; when I do that thing that I really want to do, that I know is good for my soul, even if it seems to set me back (and behind) the crowd; when I show up in the now, with my thoughts and words and deeds aligned; when I am living and laughing and learning and loving in all of that, then I know I am my authentic self.

- **Robert Wesley Branch; TV Producer & Radio Personality**

What is Authenticity? To my understanding, Authenticity is your divine characteristics. It is that thing that helps to bring forth your inner-most creativity, thoughts and expressions that are uniquely YOU. It is a state of knowing that those qualities you possess are exclusively found on the inside of you. It is arriving at a place in life where you understand that only you can identify and develop your authentic self. Authenticity can never be duplicated or replicated; it is your own personal trademark.

- DelroySouden, President and CEO of En Sound Music Awards (www.ensoundmusicawards.org)

When engaged in a dialogue about Authenticity, one will discover that Authenticity is term from the word "Authentic"; which is a methodological expression used in psychology as well as sociology, and life coaching. Authenticity is the reflection of an individual who is true to one's own personality, spirit, and character. It exposes one to the external pressures and challenges in one's life; the cognizant self is seen as coming to grips with being in a world where materialism is used as a label of value and has more credence than human life, combined with facing external trials that come with life, pressures and influences of different forms and altitudes. A lack of authenticity is a deficiency of the **REAL YOU**. I encourage you to employ the **"GET A LIFE CONCEPT"** and live authentically every day and in doing so, you will unveil your greatest potentials, talents, goals, and dreams. There is no telling what you will become or achieve when you reconnect with the AUTHENTIC YOU ~ **we all are born as ORIGINALS but most of us die as COPIES!**

   - Dr. J'Ramando Horton: Author, Executive Life Coach, Lecturer, and CEO of Bentley Coaching Institute.

Authenticity can well be described as being uncorrupted, therefore by extension of that which is real. In other words, despite being pressured, holding on to what is God-given or God-created.

- **Frankie Bobb-Semple Behavioral Change Communication Consultant, Counselor, Speechwriter, and Broadcaster.**

When you do not know who you are and your true value, it can make you vulnerable and open to anything. Many people are in debt because they over spend money to look the part of what they think others expect and will respect. Some have even endured abusive bad relationships with people who control their lives for fear of losing someone who does not even benefit their lives. It is essential that we learn who we were authentically created to be so that our identification comes from the inner being designed purposefully by God before we were born.

When we don't know who we are we will seek identification by outward sources that were only intended to be a resource and not the source of our life's purpose. Our lives should be defined by who God says we are and who He created us to be not what others think about us, what happened in our past or even what we think about ourselves. We must always remember that we are God's special beloved treasure created for greatness. The measurement of our true worth and value is the greatness God placed in the inside of us. When we recognize and embrace that authentic being, it releases us to walk in purpose and the destiny intended before we breathed our first breath.

- **Martina Young Author and Women Empowerment Specialist**

Be an original – be it in the flesh or sprit, an unaltered state of creativity and being. Our Heavenly Father never copied or duplicated the indented or master plan for creation. Our authenticity is a gift from the Master – Creator Himself to keep ourselves pure to His wishes; we can live out our earthly existence authentically.

-Jeff Franz

Authenticity is the genuineness or truth of self. Being authentically you inspires and informs, it sparks imaginations and propels destinies. It allows you and others to see that what can be imagined can merge with that which can be achieved. Each of us was created to fulfill a unique purpose and we have been empowered to take a journey of self-discovery by uncovering and unraveling depths and layers that conceal that purpose from us. As we embrace this journey and discover who we were created to be, we rise up as the authentic beings that always resided inside of each of us: ***Being Unapologetically and Authentically Me!***

Deborah Cullins-Threets, ABD, Founder and CEO Kingdom Development Institute. Doctor of Education (EDD), Argosy University, Chicago, IL

Authenticity derives from the sum of many things, beginning with a sense of who you are and having self-confidence. Everyone is unique, but our individual authenticity develops from having substantive and deep relationships with each other. To become truly authentic requires us to have spiritual partnerships and, above all, a spiritual partnership with the Divine Being. As spiritual partners we are content, demonstrate gratefulness, appreciation, and patience. These characteristics are the essence of authenticity and authentic power.

-Dwayne A, Nash JD, fifth year student and Presidential Fellow at Northwestern University Chicago IL

An Authentic Constellation

By no means am I, or the other contributors to this chapter, the only ones with a world view on authenticity. I am certain by now, after reading this book, that you have either formulated or solidified your views on what authenticity means to you. So…quickly, grab a pen so that you can also contribute to this chapter.

I (_____) believe authenticity is

_____

_____

_____

_____

_____

_____

_____

_____

Embracing Your Mark of Authenticity

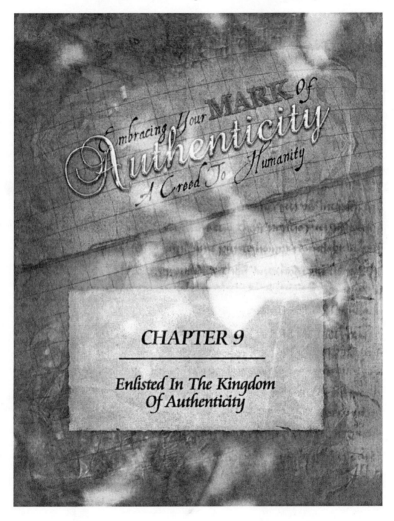

CHAPTER 9

Enlisted In The Kingdom
Of Authenticity

Embracing Your Mark of Authenticity

The Conclusion of the matter when you are enlisted in the Kingdom of Authenticity

When the Creator created the earth He knew that its sphere would be incomplete without your gifts, talents, and abilities. The total scope of your uniqueness was given to you by God – the Master Creator of the Universe. So, life lessons are just an opportunity for you to use the God-given gifts, backed by a well-developed road map, for the purpose He has deposited in you to manifest the *"Authentic You."*

Let it be known this day that Heaven has certified you as a custodian of your gifts, abilities, talents, and it will all be used to reflect the essence and reputation of your authentic worth. Whenever circumstances and/or situations arise in your life think of it is an opportunity for a practicum. This is an opportunity for you to manifest your authentic power by utilizing all the gifts, abilities, and

141

talents you already have on the inside of you. When we arise as human beings to this level of consciousness relative to our created authentic worth, maturity, splendour, and light, then we will witness the swift eradication of this global shortage of authenticity on every level of living.

When you are enlisted in the Kingdom of Authenticity and you know for sure who you are created to be and what you bring to the table of life, that same level of confident assurance will reproduce itself on the outside of you. Everyone in your immediate environment will begin to sense there's something different about you, but in a positive and distinctive way.

Don't ever be afraid to express the premium quality of what you possess on the inside to serve humanity. Reach down on the inside of you and begin to activate your authentic treasures – it's already there.

The crown and nature of being enlisted in the Kingdom of Authenticity is incumbent upon your ability to understand your purpose for living. How will you manage your gifts, talents, abilities, visions, desires, and passions in service to humanity? It's what I call "Authentic Intelligence."

Authentic intelligence is not about how powerful; affluent or well positioned you are in society. It is simply your ability to learn how to become who you already are, in conjunction with the pure service of those gifting and talents you inherently possess. This dimension of consciousness will forge a   lasting legacy of authentic living for generations to come.

If you are going to operate effectively in the Kingdom of Authenticity there are some keys which will grant you unlimited access on every level of fulfilling the specific mandate for your life. These are time-tested pillars upon which the realm of authenticity stands:

Integrity*:*

> The holistic nature of integrity has to be embraced on every level of living in the Kingdom of Authenticity.

- **Authenticity:**
  This eternal treasure "authenticity is everything in anything": to lead an inauthentic life is like rendering yourself powerless.

- **Excellence:**
  All life endeavors must be underscored with the mark of excellence.

- **Humility:**
  This is the only driving force for genuine and effective service to humanity when enlisted in the Kingdom of Authenticity.

- **Wisdom:**
  The degree of wisdom activated and applied in any given situation at any given time determines

your overall success in the Kingdom of Authenticity.

- **Character:**
Character refinement, alignment, and management are compatible to ethical and moral principles and patterns when truly enlisted in the Kingdom of Authenticity.

- **Leadership:**
The true essence of leadership resides in the ability to first identify, embrace and develop your original life's purpose. Then you can lead in the area of your proficiency.

- **Service:**
Genuine service to humanity (serving in the area of your gifts and purpose) is one of the highest honors of achievement in this lifetime, when living in the realm of authenticity.

Embracing Your Mark of Authenticity

Because you have made it to the end of this book, by default, you accepted the challenge to identify, activate, enhance, recalibrate, restate, and launch or revisit the "real you" without apology. The exuding content of the anatomy of your authenticity will now steer and keep you on a trajectory of purposeful engagement relative to your life's work. You are now in a place to continually experience the beauty of sharing your life's work with all humanity. The way you were shaped to specifically influence the temperature of your immediate atmosphere will become a constant undercurrent in your life. This level of harmonizing with who you already are will become second nature as you embrace the Mark of Authenticity on your life.

End Notes:

_____

_____

_____

_____

_____

_____

_____

_____

_____

_____

_____

_____

_____

_____

_____

_____

_____

_____

_____

_____

_____

_____

_____

_____

Embracing Your Mark of Authenticity

Another TIMELESS & POWERFUL Masterpiece!

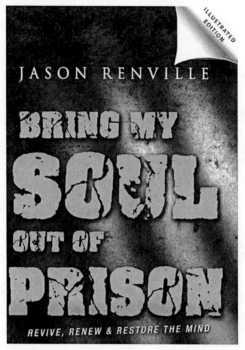

Paperback: 183 pages

Publisher: DIVINE INTELLIGENCE PRESS; 1ST edition (2008)

Language: English ISBN-10: 061533525X

ISBN-13: 978-0615335254

Meet Jason Renville

Not only the prolific author of *"Bring My Soul Out of Prison"- Revive, Renew and Renew the Mind*, and *Embracing Your Mark Of Authenticity -A Creed To Humanity,* but a sought-after empowerment facilitator: a consultant, teacher and a life coach in the areas of personal development, individual excellence, leadership and authenticity. Dr. Renville is widely regarded in the ecclesiastical arena and the Human Development market as one of the most influential facilitators in the fields of peak performance, personal and organizational building and success. His enthusiasm, sense of humor, and refreshing perspectives on "*The Authentic You*" have delighted and enlightened International and mainstream audiences in the United States. As he writes in his second book, *Embracing Your Mark of Authenticity -A Creed To Humanity.*

Renville arrived in the U. S. in 2002, in pursuit of continuing his professional studies, and with a few hundred dollars and a bag full of dreams from Guyana, South America. His accomplishments are a great example of the entrepreneurial spirit that so characterizes the fact that with a relentless focus and unwavering determination, one can accomplish the *IMPOSSIBILE.*

Through small in-house workshops on leadership and human development to life-changing events for hundreds of people, Renville has counseled people from every walk of life, from "Major Organizations" executives to educators, entrepreneurs, students, community, ecclesiastical executives, and business leaders. He has been featured on network television programs on *ATLANTA LIVE, TCT* and several radio talk Shows throughout the US where he presents his philosophy on how to achieve one's personal best and create well-balanced Authentic life. Dr. Renville is the CEO and founder of Jason Renville International, and is also the co-founder along with his wife Jenny of the Goshen Safe Haven Community Development Center for Development, Education and Empowerment (GSHCDC), an organization whose mission is to empower the community with the personal and professional development tools and strategies to achieve their personal dreams and become successful role models to future generations.

His intense researches in Strategic Organizational Leadership and Human Development have afforded him many opportunities to dialogue on the subject of leadership, authenticity, human relations, women's empowerment social reconstruction, economic development and a host of other social issues. Renville also serves as human rights representative to the United Nations.

He matriculated from institutions such as University of Guyana, Kingdom University, Chaplaincy School International in Fort Lauderdale, Florida and Bentley Coaching Institute. Renville is also a recipient of a doctorate from Florida Theological University in Theology and Counseling, where he is currently reading for another doctorate in Education with a concentration on Organizational Leadership and Sustainable Human Development.

In spite of all of these accomplishments, when asked if he regards himself as an author, speaker, entrepreneur or academician, Mr. Renville prefers to think of himself as both a coach and a cheerleader to those individuals that have accepted the challenge to become architects of their own authenticity. His work in support of the education and leadership of both the corporate and church communities has been recognized by many organizations.

His passion for his work is only surpassed by his love for his family. He currently lives in North Carolina with Jenny, his wife of 11 years and his three children, Victoria, Judah and Jason.

Embracing Your Mark of Authenticity